MW00577379

St. Johns
River Guidebook

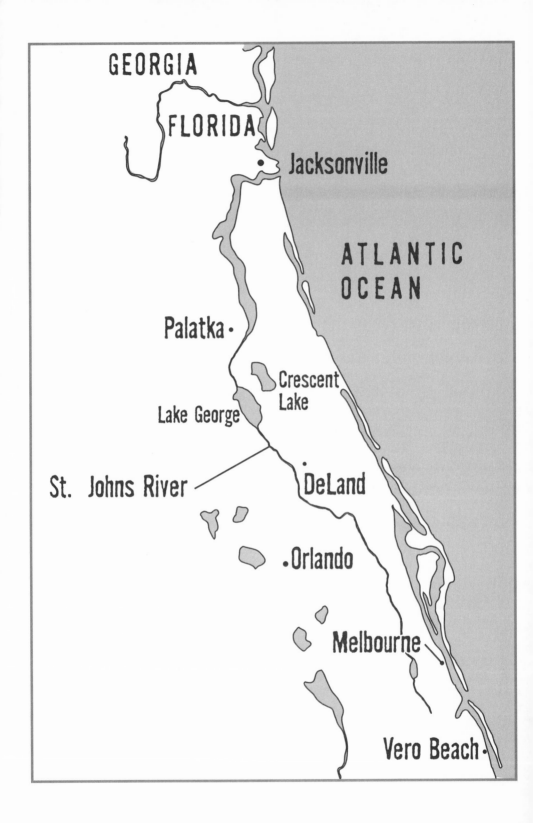

St. Johns
River Guidebook

Kevin M. McCarthy

Pineapple Press, Inc.
Sarasota, Florida

Inquiries should be addressed to:

Pineapple Press, Inc.
P.O. Box 3889
Sarasota, Florida 34230

www.pineapplepress.com

Photo on p. 109 courtesy of Amanda Smith, *osprey*design.
Photos and illustrations on pp 4, 7, 11, 16, 14, 31, 58, 79, 98, 106, and 120 courtesy of the Florida Archives and the Florida Photographic Collection.
All other photos by the author.

Library of Congress Cataloging-in-Publication Data

McCarthy, Kevin.
  St. Johns River guidebook / by Kevin M. McCarthy.-- 1st ed.
     p. cm.
  Includes bibliographical references and index.
  ISBN 1-56164-314-9 (pb : alk. paper)
  1. Saint Johns River (Fla.)--Guidebooks. 2. Saint Johns River Valley (Fla.)--Guidebooks. I. Title: Saint Johns River guidebook. II. Title.

  F317.S2M38 2004
  917.59'10464--dc22
                                2004013992

First Edition
10 9 8 7 6 5 4 3 2 1

Design by *osprey*design
Printed in the United States of America

Contents

Dedication

I dedicate this book to the many members of the Marjorie Kinnan Rawlings Society for helping to preserve the rural Florida that Mrs. Rawlings wrote about so well; and to my children (Katie, Brendan, Erin, and Matt) that they may do their part in preserving and enjoying the river, lakes, and bays of this great state.

Acknowledgments

I wish to thank computer expert Vilija Baublyte, John Clark, Jena Counts, Dr. James Cusick, airboat guide John "Wes" Dinkins, cartographer Susan Duser, Pat and Dale Garlinghouse, Pat Hite, Karen Jacobs, Jake Jacoway, computer expert Justin Johnson, Jeff King, photographer John Knaub, Guerry McClellan, Dr. Jerald Milanich, Jerry Moldrik, Joann Mossa, Dick Neusch, Steve Nichols, David Nolan, Dr. Gordon Patterson, Dale Potts, Molinda Prevatt, Dr. Barbara Purdy, Mary Solomonson, Harmon Williams, and Ronald Williamson. Also thanks to the unknown boaters who kindly directed my two boating companions and me out of water hyacinths and deadends. Finally, a special thanks to Edwina and Bob Davis for inviting me along on a very memorable trip down the St. Johns in their boat.

About the Author

Kevin M. McCarthy is a professor of English and Florida Studies at the University of Florida in Gainesville. He has written ten other books for Pineaple Press, including *African Americans in Florida, Alligator Tales, Aviation in Florida, Book Lover's Guide to Florida, Christmas in Florida, Georgia's Lighthouses and Historic Coastal Sites, Guide to the University of Florida and Gainesville, Native Americans in Florida, Thirty Florida Shipwrecks,* and *Twenty Florida Pirates.*

How to Use This Book

The first part of each chapter, "By Water," describes the trip boating along from one section of the river to the next, each ending at a good stopping place for the night. I briefly describe my experiences and then tell of the history and natural history of that area of the river. The last part of each chapter, "By Land," tells you about that same section if you are going along the river by land in a car. The "By Land" sections are much shorter, so even if you are going by car, you need to read the "By Water" sections to get all the history and background.

The Appendices, "Information for Boaters," and "Places to Visit, Stay, and Eat," contain all the general, practical hints as well as information on food and lodging and tourist sites. It seemed better to put all this together for your touring convenience.

Introduction

From any point of view—historical, commercial, or recreational—the St. Johns River is the most important river in Florida. Its 310 miles have been witness to some of the most important people in our state's history: Jean Ribault, John and William Bartram, John McIntosh, Zephaniah Kingsley, Harriet Beecher Stowe; as well as many important groups: Timucuan and Seminole Indians, runaway slaves, British and Spanish settlers, missionaries, and many thousands of more modern Floridians and visitors who have boated, fished, developed, painted, photographed, and described the river. It has attracted more than its share of get-rich-quick schemers who are more interested in exploitation than preservation. But the St. Johns also attracts an increasing number of people who want to explore its history and nature, and who want to protect it from despoilers in order to preserve it for the future.

In many ways, the history of the river parallels that of the people of Florida: the Native Americans who lived in many settlements along the river and used it for transportation; the French and Spanish who fought on the river for domination of the whole peninsula; the runaway slaves who used it to seek freedom; the early tourists who frequented the river to find relief from northern winters; the settlers along its banks looking to find a new beginning to raise their families and earn a living; the modern residents who come for the river's commerce and recreation.

The St. Johns bisects or skirts twelve Florida counties, including three of the state's biggest: Orange, Volusia, and Duval. And although it offers excellent fishing and boating prospects, because it is located west of the popular Atlantic coast it has been spared some of the onslaught of the incessant development that has characterized Florida in the last fifty years.

This is primarily a guidebook to the river from its source in the swamps west of Vero Beach to the mouth of the St. Johns at Mayport. It describes the history, major towns/cities along the way, personages associated with the river, prospects for its future, and potential problem areas. Because not everyone interested in the river has the time or facilities to boat it, the last part of each chapter describes the land part on each side of the St. Johns, from south to north. The last chapter contains the names and description of some of the many places of lodging and eating along the river.

This was a fun book to write. For the research part I read as many articles and books that I could find about the river. Then I boated most of the navigable river, north from Lake Harney (east-northeast of Orlando), up to the Atlantic Ocean off Mayport, then south by airboat from west of Melbourne to the beginnings of the river. For the land part, I drove up and down both sides of the river from Mayport to Highway 192, stopping at fish camps, motels, restaurants, bait stores, not only to find the practical information boaters/drivers might want about where to eat or stay, but also to get a sense of the river in the lives of those who make a living, even indirectly, from it.

Many kinds of vessels ply the river: large-boat operators and fishermen make a living from it, day trippers use it to spend delightful days meandering along its nooks and crannies, and houseboaters either anchor along the banks or go slowly up and down. The river has many spectacular places. You may see manatees and jumping fish and lots of species of birds. On quiet weekdays, you will experience a solitude and closeness to nature that may surprise you in this very populated state. Even on busy weekends, you can find pockets of quiet, although they are increasingly more difficult to find, especially as you approach Jacksonville.

So come aboard. Put on your hat and throw away your cares. Let's float down the St. Johns (though for this north-flowing river, down is up!). We'll start where the river starts, in the marshes west of Vero Beach, and end up at the Atlantic Ocean.

1

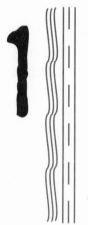

St. Johns Marsh
to
Lake Monroe

"When we looked over our shoulders,

the marsh had closed in over the

channel by which we had come. We

were in a labyrinth. The stretch of

open water was merely the fluid

heart of a maze."

—Marjorie Kinnan Rawlings
describing a trip on the St. Johns

by water to Lake Monroe

There oughta be a sign where a river begins: "This is where the St. Johns (or Mississippi or Thames) begins." It would save so much time and trouble traipsing, in my case, through a swamp, looking for tiny rivulets that could be identified as the headwaters of the river. It would make things definite, just the way the jetty at Mayport signals the end of the river and the place where the Atlantic Ocean takes over.

Somewhere west of Vero Beach is the beginning of the St. Johns River. Exactly where, no one can say with certainty. Probably someplace in the St. Johns Marsh. There, tiny streams begin to join others, flowing ever so slowly to the north, never really gaining much speed even by the time they reach the Atlantic Ocean at Mayport. The river falls very, very slowly, about an inch per mile over its 310-mile length. Most of the St. Johns is surprisingly narrow, although it can reach over a mile wide around Palatka. At times, it can be very difficult to determine exactly in which direction the main current flows since it never gains a lot of speed and there are so many offstreams and sidetracks.

So why does the St. Johns flow north? There are two reasons. First is the drainage from locally high topography on the Lake Wales Ridge in central Florida. Second is the effect of ancient and modern barrier islands that lie parallel to the coast east of the river. In fact, although the river has a large drainage basin, it has a low discharge and could almost be considered a tidal lake. It actually has two tides a day as far south as Astor.

So we begin our trip west of Vero Beach where the St. Johns Marsh and the likely beginnings of the St. Johns River are. When I ventured into the southern part of the St. Johns with two boating companions, the lack of channel markers was maddeningly frustrating; we were completely lost several times. We tried doing what Marjorie Kinnan Rawlings, author of such works as *South Moon Under* (1933), the Pulitzer Prize–winning novel *The Yearling* (1938), and *Cross Creek* (1942), did when she boated on the St. Johns in 1933: follow the direction of the water hyacynths as they float north. Other times, we had to ask a fisherman on the bank ("Where's the main channel?") or follow those who seemed to know where they were going.

The ever-present water hyacinth (*Eichhornia crassipes*) that boaters see along the St. Johns is actually considered one of the worst weeds in the

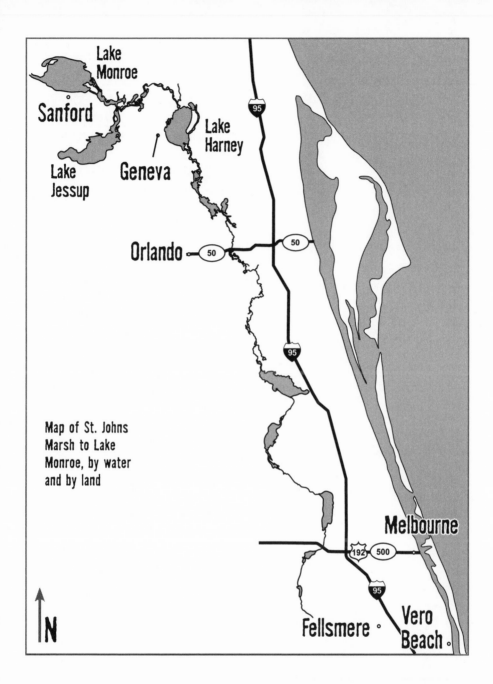

Map of St. Johns
Marsh to Lake
Monroe, by water
and by land

N

world. How it came to pervade Florida waters, including the St. Johns, can probably be traced back to a Mrs. W.W. Fuller of Palatka. She obtained a few samples of the South American plant, which had hitherto been unknown in the United States, at the 1884 World's Industrial and Cotton

Centennial Exposition in New Orleans. With its disarmingly romantic name and purple flowers that resembled the orchid's, the water hyacinth became a hit.

Mrs. Fuller, who owned a winter home at Edgewater near San Mateo southeast of Palatka, put small offshoots of the hyacinth into the St. Johns to beautify the river near her home. Within ten years, those few offshoots proliferated to cover fifty million acres of the river and its tributaries. Cattlemen took it into more streams to feed their cattle, not realizing that the plant provides very little nutrition to the animals. The plant grew so rapidly that it impeded boat traffic on the river and threatened the commercial usefulness of the St. Johns. The federal government ended up spending more than $500,000 in the four decades since 1890 trying to eradicate it, to no avail.

Until rather recently, the hyacinth was a major problem on the rivers and lakes of Florida. Not only did it block boat traffic and prevent swimming and fishing, but infestations of the plant prevented sunlight and oxygen from penetrating the water. Such infestations depleted fish populations, shaded out submerged plants, and reduced biological diversity. Finally, though, in the last decade or so, years of coordinated efforts by local, state, and federal water managers have managed to control the pest and keep it at low levels by using herbicides, machines, and biocontrol insects. The water hyacinth is just one of many non-native plants that have plagued Florida. Many unsuspecting people have disposed of so-called exotics in waterways or forests, only to have the non-indigenous throwaways thrive in this state's climate.

Water hyacinth and weeds have clogged the river's length throughout its history.

Although one can take a shallow-draft boat up the St. Johns when it is flowing well and deep, and some fishermen can be found using outboard motorboats, the preferred means of transport, especially off the main part of the river, is the airboat. Officials used to allow

Wes Dinkins and the author head off south to the start of the river.

swamp buggies (strange-looking vehicles with huge balloon tires, gun racks, and maybe a place to hold some favorite home-brewed beverage), but such vehicles caused too much damage and are no longer allowed.

I decided to try something different on my quest for the beginnings of the St. Johns. I went with river tour-guide John "Wes" Dinkins on an airboat from the first accessible camp, Camp Holly, where the river goes under Highway 192/500. We went about one hour south through Sawgrass Lake, Little Sawgrass Lake, and then Lake Hell 'n Blazes until the river narrowed and petered out into the swamp.

At the place where we began our airboat trip south, I could see remnants of an old wooden bridge which had been replaced with a concrete one in order to handle the heavier traffic. I was to find out that day and also later, during much of our trip north, how relatively quiet the river is, except for the sounds of nature, compared to the busy bridges over the river and many of the roads along its banks, especially on weekdays. True, the boat traffic picks up noticeably on weekends, but those who can boat and fish the river during the week can have much of the river to themselves.

When I asked Wes for his theory on the origin of the name of Lake Hell 'n Blazes, he said that in the early twentieth century, when the islands were free-floating and not anchored, it was very difficult and confusing to navigate the river there, which would bring out a string of words like "hell" and "blazes" from the boaters. To such people, the river seemed to change direction depending on where the islands were. Some of the more squeamish have euphemized the name to Lake Helen Blazes, but most maps have it as Hell 'n Blazes.

A guide like Wes can point out spots of historical significance along the river, such as places where Native Americans used to hunt and camp (for example, at Indian Mound), where local loggers have cut straight channels through the swamp in order to float out the huge cypresses, where workers built canals to drain the land, or where the Union Cypress Railroad used to access the interior, especially the groves of large trees, to haul cypress trees to the sawmill in Hopkins (present-day South Melbourne).

The scenery south of Lake Hell 'n Blazes is really spectacular. No place on the river has such a variety and number of alligators, anhingas, ibises, great blue herons, turtles, and other wildlife. We happened to go through during alligator-hunting season, during which hunters who have won "the lottery" (the permit given out by lottery to a "lucky" few) can go out, usually at night, looking to kill alligators which they can more easily spot when powerful searchlights sweeping the banks pick up the telltale pairs of eyes. The airboaters camp out on some of the hammocks. Controlled kills are necessary to check the growing number of gators.

The beginning of the river is very isolated, but spectacular in beauty.

Off to the west are Jane Green Creek and Jane Green Swamp, supposedly named after a woman who became lost in the area many years ago and was never heard from again. According to my guide, people could hear her screaming but couldn't find her. Local guides can point out a so-called "secret passage" to the Jane Green Creek on the west bank about two thirds of the way down the channel between Little Sawgrass Lake and Hell 'n Blazes. During droughts the low-water level necessitates taking an airboat to the creek.

Florida's Cypress Union Company loggers in 1916.

The St. Johns Marsh is vast. Developers once thought it could be drained, that the land could be claimed for agriculture, and that towns/cities could be built to accommodate the throngs of people wanting to live in south Florida. Hamilton Disston bought four million acres of South Florida swamp for twenty-five cents an acre in 1881 and then drained much of it, before the economic panic of 1893 ended that venture. He would not be the last to come along with grandiose plans of draining Florida swamps to make more land for agriculture, housing developments, theme parks, and more and more people.

W.W. Russell of Cincinnati bought 115,000 acres west of Sebastian from the United States Printing Company in 1895. He planned on draining the St. Johns Marsh, convinced that the elevation of the land would allow the project to be accomplished relatively inexpensively. He also planned on building a railroad from Sebastian into the marsh. That project ended with the death of Russell in 1900.

Napoleon Bonaparte Broward, who served as Florida governor from 1905 to 1909, was one of those who planned to drain the Everglades farther south and produce more arable land; that plan may have encouraged developers along the St. Johns to do likewise. Another ambitious drainage proponent was Nelson Fell, who planned to drain 118,000 acres at the headwaters of the St. Johns, sell the retrieved land to would-be farmers, and become rich in the process. He helped found the town of Fellsmere, a name that combined his own with "mere," meaning "a great watery place." He too failed due to a combination of factors: plans that were too ambitious, the outbreak of World War I in 1914, torrential downpours that flooded the retrieved land, and a growing economic malaise affecting this country. You can still see some of the thirty-three miles of levies, sixty-seven miles of canals, and 215 miles of drainage ditches his company built.

West of Fellsmere was the colony of Broadmoor, which a group of Dutch investors established in 1912. Truck crops and basic farming provided a decent income to the residents, but a torrential downpour in 1915 which dumped thirteen inches of rain within twenty-four hours flooded the town and forced the people to leave. The town never recovered.

Early developers managed to drain about seventy percent of the marsh along the upper St. Johns. They thought they were "reclaiming" the land for agricultural and urban use, but their misguided efforts caused there to be much less water in the upper basin of the river during the dry season and then sudden and deeper flood stages during the wet season. Decreased water levels in the marsh also led to a reduction in the number of fish. The depletion of oxygen caused by decaying organic matter washing into the mainstream, a flow that would have been stopped if the marshlands had been allowed to remain, also resulted in massive fish kills.

From 1900 to 1970, developers drained as much as 300,000 acres of the Upper St. Johns River Basin. Strong floods did a lot of damage in the 1920s and 1940s. Wildlife left for greener pastures, and the shellfish and fishing industries along the Indian River Lagoon were drastically changed by the diversion of an immense amount of fresh water into the estuary from the St. Johns. And still, engineers wanted to drain more land and send more water to the Indian River.

Finally, in the last three decades environmentalists have convinced authorities of how foolish those drainage projects were in the long run. A huge restoration project, which was begun in 1988 and which some have called the largest marsh restoration project in our country's history, has reversed the trend to get rid of the swamp in Indian River and Brevard Counties. The results are promising: more than 150,000 acres of marsh in those counties have been restored; reservoirs have been built to contain the nutrient-rich runoff from farms before it can drain into the St. Johns or Indian rivers; wildlife, including birds and fish, are returning; and plant life is once again doing well in the area.

One of the guardians of the river is The St. Johns River Water Management District (SJRWMD), which the Florida Legislature established in 1972 as one of five districts dedicated to the preservation and management of Florida's precious water resources. The SJRWMD manages ground and surface water supplies in eighteen counties in northeast and east-central Florida. It has more than seven hundred staff members and several main functions: to issue permits for various water use activities and/or activities that have the potential to damage ground or surface water resources and adjacent lands, to buy land to preserve or restore vital wetlands and water resources, to conduct research about the quality and quantity of ground and surface water resources, to map ground and surface water resources, and to conduct outreach and public education programs.

The SJRWMD has bought much of the land on each side of the river and will preserve it. The farmers used to pump their water into the river, but the fertilizers in it polluted the river. Now they pump the water into reservoirs to purify it before putting it into the river. A $2 million dredging project to clean Hell 'n Blazes and Sawgrass of their pollution-laden muck is meant to purify the water before it moves downstream into Lake Washington, one of the main sources of drinking water for some 200,000 people living in cities in and around Melbourne on the coast. The muck has had fifty years to decrease oxygen levels in the lakes, cut down fish populations, and damage water quality.

South of Hell 'n Blazes is the Three Forks Marsh Conservation Area, fifty-two thousand acres of marshlands beginning where the river forks into three small branches—hence the name of the conservation area. Engineers have built there a vast network of levees to collect the water runoff from neighboring agricultural lands. The area has campsites that are accessible only by boat (see chapter 10 for visiting information).

Workers built a road and levee between 1910 and 1914 that cut off the St. Johns and Blue Cypress Lake from their headwater marshes. This, added to the reclamation of land for agriculture, the channelization of the river (so that today more than seventy percent of the basin is used for cattle production), and the huge reduction of marshes and swamps feeding the river altered the St. Johns floodplain dramatically. The resulting change in the grasses from sawgrass marshes to cordgrass and woody species has greatly reduced the number of waterfowl and wading bird populations in the area.

Having explored the beginnings of the St. Johns, we continue by following its northbound flow towards Lake Monroe. North of Sawgrass Lake and Highways 192/500, the St. Johns flows into Lakes Washington, Winder, and Poinsett (named for Joel Robert Poinsett, special envoy and American minister to Mexico in the early 1820s, who introduced to the United States the colorful plant known as the poinsettia). In the early 1900s, a developer, George Hopkins, began to drain the upper fifty miles of the river, marsh, and lakes in order to plant profitable cash crops like indigo and a type of cane. His workers began building by hand a canal between Lake Washington and Eau Gallie River toward the east coast. The hardness of the ground eventually stopped them, although they tried to get a steam trencher to complete the job. Fortunately, the U.S. Army Corps of Engineers stopped the drainage work.

The river meanders north throughout the length of Brevard County, basically paralleling I-95, one of the busiest interstates in the nation. Very few of the motorists speeding by are aware of the river slowly heading north beside them. On the other side of I-95, of course, is the fast-growing Atlantic coast of Florida, almost a megalopolis from Miami to Jacksonville. To the immediate east is the futuristic Cape Kennedy/Cape Canaveral area, one of the first areas that Spanish explorers like Ponce de León saw in the early 1500s.

Boaters can find huts like this one at the beginning of the river where they can find shelter during a storm.

North of Lake Poinsett the St. Johns borders the eastern part of the William Beardall Tosohatchee State Reserve, a 28,000-acre park.

Established in 1977 under Florida's Environmentally Endangered Lands program, the park helps preserve the extensive wetlands that are essential for the cleansing of the St. Johns. At this point the river serves as the border between Brevard and Orange Counties and goes under the Beeline Expressway (SR 528), the aptly named road that takes motorists between Orlando and the Cocoa area.

North of that, where SR 50 crosses over the river, is where Marjorie Kinnan Rawlings began a memorable ten-day trip in 1933 with her friend Dessie Smith. Rawlings had been in a real funk before the trip. Her marriage to Charles Rawlings was deteriorating, life seemed oppressive, and—as she wrote in the "Hyacinth Drift" chapter of *Cross Creek*—she felt she "had hardships that seemed . . . more than one could bear alone." Like thousands of others over the years, she took to the water, in this case a river, to forget her troubles for a while and worry about more manageable problems like catching fish for dinner, keeping the mosquitoes away, and finding the main channel.

Marjorie Kinnan Rawlings at her Cross Creek home in the 1930s.

In 1995, two women friends of mine retraced the path that Rawlings and Smith had taken sixty-two years earlier. After discussing the trip with eighty-eight-year-old Dessie Smith at her home in Crystal River, they embarked, following the same route as the earlier women and having some of the same experiences, especially meeting those who live along the river or make their living from it: independent individuals more at home with a fishing pole or frog-gigger than a laptop or cell phone.

Just north of Puzzle Lake is where the Econlockhatchee River enters the St. Johns and helps to increase its volume heading north. That river and the Wekiva further north come from Central Florida, with its teeming population and theme parks and spreading urbanization. The result, up until the mid-1990s, was a massive influx of stormwater runoff and treated sewage into the St. Johns River. As much as thirty-five million gallons of treated sewage were entering the river each day, resulting in large amounts of blue-green algae, which caused huge fish kills in the 1970s and 1980s. Since then a regional wastewater treatment plant near Orlando has reduced the amount of nitrogen and phosphorus entering the St. Johns. The policing of the river by concerned groups has also helped, but the burgeoning population growth in Central Florida threatens to overwhelm the system and do irreparable damage to the river.

Near where Brevard, Orange, and Volusia Counties come together, the river begins heading north-northwest into Seminole County and up into Lake Harney, which is named after Colonel (later General) William Selby Harney, who defeated the Seminoles in the 1830s near Homestead, Florida. Lakes Harney, Jesup, and several others along the St. Johns are named after federal officers who served during the Seminole Indian Wars, indicating how important the river was for the transportation of troops and cargoes in that era.

Lake Harney is where I actually boarded my friends' boat to make the trip to Mayport, mostly because the depth of the river was about two feet below normal. South of this point in 2003 it was simply too shallow to launch anything but a kayak or a very shallow-draft boat or an airboat. Getting into Lake Harney from the C.S. Lee Park at SR 46 is very difficult, as evidenced by our running aground several times near Cow Island. We finally asked a local boater if we could follow him out the winding, unmarked channel. Increasing our speed and planing over the water, which raised our motor, helped, but the lack of markers leading to the lake makes for a difficult time, especially for boaters unaccustomed to the area.

As my own two river companions and I, all members of the Marjorie Kinnan Rawlings Society, headed north, we tried to guess where Rawlings and Smith camped each night, encountered strangers, or stopped to look at the scenery. In fact, we had with us Rawlings's "Hyacinth Drift" chapter, as well as William Bartram's travelogue.

Lake Harney is a little over nine square miles in size, but very shallow. Even once on the lake, finding our way out of it into the river heading north is not easy. (We followed a speeding local boater who knew the channel well.) We saw very few people on and around the lake, but the view of scattered houses along the lake will probably become more congested as city-dwellers head for relatively isolated waterside regions like this.

On the western shore of the lake two miles from present-day Geneva was the site of a Seminole Indian War outpost, Fort Lane, named after Lieutenant Colonel John Lane, who died in Florida in 1836. Federal troops used the fort during the Second Seminole War (1835–1842), but the site of the fort has long since been abandoned and taken back by the surrounding woods. (More details about the fort are in the land tour that follows.) One can still see in the Geneva Historical Society building to the west a few remnants of that fort.

Lake Harney was the place on the St. Johns that Confederate Secretary of War John Breckinridge reached during his successful escape from the United States in 1865 at the end of the Civil War. After arriving at present-day Astor on the St. Johns, he was assisted by three men under the command of Captain J.J. Dickison. Using a small boat they had salvaged from the sunken Union boat *Columbine* (see chapter five for more details), the three men took their escaping dignitary up the river for four days until they reached Lake Harney. They then took Breckinridge cross-country to the Indian River, which he sailed down and eventually escaped, making his way to Cuba and then England. On that trip, the mosquitoes were so bad that the escaping party would anchor in the middle of the St. Johns each evening to try to avoid the swarms of bugs on the river bank.

East of Lake Harney is Volusia County, while Seminole County is on the west. As you leave the lake and meander north-northwest to Lake Monroe, you pass on the left the abandoned Osceola Airfield. Many such airfields were built during World War II, and while some became the main airports for growing towns after the war, others were soon abandoned and left to nature.

A might-have-been that would have dramatically affected Lake Harney and the St. Johns was the plan in the mid-1960s to build a canal between the St. Johns and Indian Rivers near the Atlantic coast. The St. Johns–Indian River Barge Canal, which would have been the southern exit of the infamous Cross Florida Barge Canal (see chapter five), was to link the Gulf of Mexico with the space complex at Cape Canaveral. The canal across Volusia County would have been 150 feet wide and twelve feet deep, beginning at Lake Monroe near Sanford, heading south past Lake Jesup, and leaving the southern part of Lake Harney into a 250-foot lifting lock. Planners noted that, besides huge barges, 25,000 pleasure boats would use the St. Johns and new canal each year, all of which would have a major, certainly negative, impact on the river. When President Nixon finally halted the Cross Florida Barge Canal in 1971, that effectively stopped the St. Johns–Indian River Barge Canal proposal, much to the satisfaction of environmentalists.

Even above Lake Harney all the way to Lake Monroe the river can be difficult to navigate since there are very few directional signs. The maps are unclear, especially with the many side channels that lead nowhere. Clue: get several maps, follow local boaters, and ask for directions. The section from Lake Harney to Lake Monroe is one of the most beautiful and isolated of the whole river, especially on weekdays. From time to time, especially on weekends, the cacophony of speeding airboats and airplanes overhead will shatter the quiet, send animals scurrying, and make you wish there were some way to muffle the engines.

When the river leaves Lake Harney and continues its meandering in a north-northwest direction in Seminole County, it passes by the settlement of Osceola (named after the Seminole leader), Palm Shadows, and Indian Mound Village.

To the right about a half-mile down the river from the entrance to Lake Harney is Deep Creek, a five-mile-long waterway that leads to Lake Ashby via Lake Ashby Canal. Although difficult for boats to navigate, the creek is good for fishing, as are many of the creeks that come into the main river. This particular creek was probably the site of Native American villages two hundred years ago. Off to the right are lakes with descriptive names like Mud and Mullet and Thornhill. They are usually accessible from the St. Johns, depending on drought conditions.

The section of the river between Lake Harney and Lake Monroe is one of the prettiest sections on the whole river simply because it has fewer signs of habitation and more alligators, turtles, and birds. As is true of much of the area along the river, one can see here different kinds of houses and architectural styles, from the weekend shack to the mansion.

Just before the river enters Lake Monroe, it goes under Highway 46 twice. As it does so, it skirts the northeastern edge of a large body of water, Lake Jesup, a sixteen-square-mile lake named after a Second Seminole War federal officer. Steamboats used to go to and from the lake in the nineteenth century and had four landings where they could discharge and take on passengers and cargo. Highway 417 crosses the lake as part of the Central Florida Greenway.

Just where the Highway 46 bridge crosses the St. Johns is the Sanford Boat Works, where one can go on eco-tours around the area. The bridge over the river, the Douglas Stenstrom Bridge, honors a state senator from 1954 to 1959 who worked to have the bridge built to replace an old wooden span that now serves as a fishing pier. Just before entering Lake Monroe, you can see to the left (west) a Native American mound after which Indian Mound Village is named.

As we approach the southern end of Lake Monroe, we say goodbye to the most isolated part of the river and head to increasingly busy stretches—although the river will still have patches of isolation.

by land to Lake Monroe

No highways on either side of the river follow its winding path, but one can reach fish camps and trailer parks by taking smaller roads from the main highways. The area south of Lake Harney is impassable to cars within the vicinity of the St. Johns, and four-wheel drive vehicles are necessary for off-the-road trips along the river.

One can, however, drive along the western edge of the river near Osceola. About four miles west on Highway 46 is the small town of Geneva, probably named after a local resident, the wife of a railroadman from New Geneva, New York, although some gazetteers think the name may go back to the city in Switzerland. Its original name, Harney Cove, stressed its nearness to Lake Harney. A railroad from Lake Okeechobee to the Florida east coast passed through Geneva until the 1940s, when the line was abandoned.

Of possible interest to Civil War buffs is the Geneva Cemetery, located at the end of 0.4-mile Cemetery Road, which is .3 miles east of the junction of Highways 46 and 426. The cemetery has the graves of seventeen Civil War soldiers: fifteen Confederate and two Union. Also buried there is the skull of Lewis Thornton Powell, who, as part of the conspiracy to assassinate President Lincoln and government officials in April 1865, tried to kill Secretary of State William Seward. Although his attempt to stab Seward to death did not succeed, Powell was captured, tried, and hanged for his part in the crime. Powell's body has been lost, but his skull was discovered in the Smithsonian Institution and returned to his family members, some of whom were living in Geneva, and they buried it there.

Lewis Thornton Powell, and the resting place of his skull.

PVT. LEWIS THORNTON POWELL, CSA
APRIL 22, 1844 – JULY 7, 1865
2ND FLORIDA INFANTRY, CO. I
"HAMILTON BLUES"
43RD BATTALION VIRGINIA CALVARY
"MOSBYS RANGERS"

To reach the actual gravesite, from the entrance of the cemetery walk forty-four yards down the center path, then twenty-five yards to the right, then six yards to the right.

The Museum of Geneva History is just east of the junction of Highways 46 and 426 (see chapter ten for phone number and hours). The museum has artifacts from Fort Lane, which was on the western shore of Lake Harney. To reach the site of the fort, from the intersection of Highways 46 and 426, drive .6 miles east, turn right on Lake Geneva Road and go .8 miles, turn left on Lake Harney Road and go 1.2 miles, turn right on Jungle Road and go .9 miles, turn left on Fort Lane Road, and then go .4 miles to Fort Lane Park on the left.

Visitors can find in the pavilion at the park a small sheet describing a "History Hike" they can take around the park. Markers throughout the park point to the presence of a Native American midden, a log from Fort Lane, a crosstie from the railroad that served Geneva from 1912 until 1942, and possibly part of an airplane that crashed into a tree on an unsuccessful landing at a nearby grassy runway.

Residents of Geneva used to make the thirty-mile boat trip to Sanford on the St. Johns, but a primitive road built in 1910 cut the time and distance considerably. The road was paved with brick in 1917. Workers built SR 46 of sand and oil in 1946.

North of the town and Lake Geneva, Osceola Road East leads past the abandoned Osceola Airfield to the town of Osceola near the St. Johns after it leaves Lake Harney. Drivers can reach Osceola by taking Avenue C in Geneva to Old Geneva Road to West Osceola Road, or by going ten miles east from SR 46 on Osceola Road, first west, then east. Osceola Road winds around near the west bank of the St. Johns to a dead end, but the houses along the river block its view from the road.

During the Second Seminole War in the 1830s, two Seminole leaders, King Philip and his son, Coacoochee, had a camp in the vicinity of Osceola, which the U.S. military named King Philipstown. Twenty years later, in the 1850s, a man named Cook operated a ferry there across the St. Johns, giving rise to the new place name, Cook's Ferry. That ferry, poled across and guided by submerged cables, was one of four along the river. The site became known as Osceola in 1916–1918, when the Osceola Cypress Company began extracting the valuable trees from the Lake Okeechobee area, taking them to Osceola by a new railroad, and shipping them north.

Osceola is the most widespread place name in Florida that commemorates a Native American. Part Creek, part Scots, Osceola was the most famous leader of the Seminoles, both for how he spurned the whites and how he died. Although not a chief of the Seminoles through heredity, he was a war leader through his appeal and bravery. A well-known story about Osceola states that he thrust his knife through a treaty that federal officials were trying to convince the Seminoles to sign. The story's accuracy is not known, but it reflects how the leader was seen.

Osceola coordinated attacks on federal troops, both at Fort King near present-day Ocala and on the road from Fort Brooke in Tampa to Fort King. The latter massacre resulted in the deaths of dozens at a place now known as Dade Battlefield State Park. In 1837, General Jesup captured Osceola outside St. Augustine under a white flag of truce and imprisoned him and many of his followers in the Castillo de San Marcos in St. Augustine. While the others eventually escaped from the prison, Osceola, either because he was too weak from disease or too dispirited and angry at the whites, did not. He was taken to Fort Moultrie in South Carolina, where he died in 1838.

The town of Osceola grew up as a cypress mill town in the first part of the twentieth century. As many as two hundred men worked the mill there, and the Osceola Cypress Company took out thousands of trees from the surrounding wetlands. As so often happened in the history of this state, once the company had extracted all the useful cypress trees, it packed up and left, oblivious to the possibility of replanting seedlings.

Today all that is left of the mill is a windowless brick vault. A surviving bald cypress tree that was spared is called the Senator and is still visible from the St. Johns though it stands eight miles away in Big Tree Park off U.S. Highway 17-92 in Seminole County's Spring Hammock preserve.

The surrounding forest provided jobs for local residents, especially in the sawmills and turpentine camps. Although most of the trees were cut in such sawmills, some of the logs were floated down the river to Jackson-ville. The turpentine industry, which closed locally in 1927, employed three hundred workers and built eighty buildings, which included living accommodations and work facilities.

The windowless brick vault is all that is left of a sawmill.

2 Sanford to Hontoon Island

"Faunally speaking, the St. Johns River is an extraordinary stream, like no other in America. Its most distinctive feature is the degree to which marine animals of diverse kinds and divergent ways of life either live there permanently or seasonally ascend the river."

—*Archie Carr,* A Naturalist in Florida: A Celebration of Eden

by water from Sanford to Hontoon Island

The upper (southern) part of the St. Johns, especially below Hontoon Island, has an unspoiled beauty, partly because much of the undeveloped land on either side is owned by county, state, or federal agencies that plan to keep it that way forever. Not only do these peaceful, uninhabited stretches evoke what Florida must have looked like before European explorers began arriving in the sixteenth century, they also reveal why Florida's image in the nineteenth century was one of idyllic beauty. Writers like Sidney Lanier, Ralph Waldo Emerson, and Harriet Beecher Stowe had many kind words to write about the Sunshine State, which probably attracted many visitors and would-be residents.

As schoolchildren know from their history classes, Florida was the first territory of the North American mainland that European explorers reached in the sixteenth century, but the last of the land on the east coast of the United States to be developed. That is due in part to the fact that the Spanish, who controlled it, never put too much time and energy into colonizing it, other than to have a few outposts like St. Augustine that could be called upon to protect the Spanish treasure fleets sailing back to Spain from the Caribbean. Also, until the advent in the twentieth century of air-conditioning, mosquito control, and roads that made the peninsula fully accessible to drivers, Florida remained a relative frontier.

As boaters make their way into Lake Monroe from the south, they go around or near a pair of encircling peninsulas named "Mothers Arms." The lake is fairly large (9,406 acres) and drains some 2,420 square miles in the area, but is surprisingly shallow, reaching only seven to eight feet in the center. The lake has had several names: Wepolokse (Round Lake) to the Seminoles, Valdez to the Spanish, and Monroe to the Americans (in honor of the fifth U.S. president, James Monroe). The lake is divided between Volusia and Seminole Counties.

In the first quarter of the nineteenth century, Seminoles were living around the lake, raising cattle descended from those left behind by the Spanish and farming the land with methods taught them by escaped slaves from Carolina and Georgia plantations. As white settlers moved into central Florida and encountered resistance from the Native Americans, the federal government sent in troops to kill or capture them and send them to Indian Territory in the West.

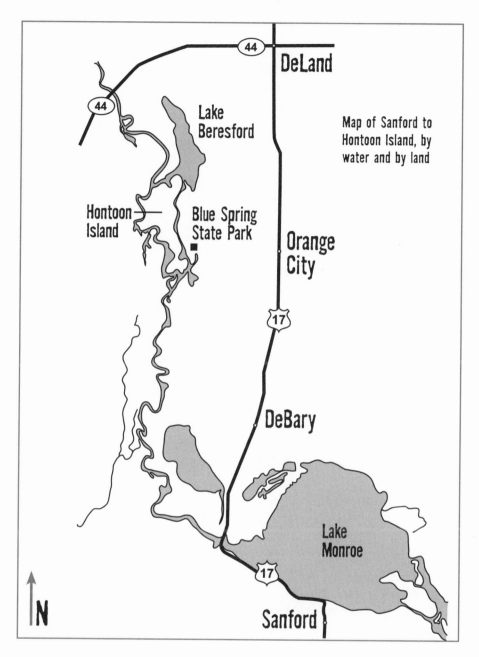

Map of Sanford to Hontoon Island, by water and by land

In 1837, Colonel William Harney, after whom Lake Harney was named, established Camp Monroe on the southern shore of Lake Monroe. On February 8, two hundred Seminoles, led by King Philip and his son, Coacoochee, attacked the soldiers at the camp and killed the officer in charge, Captain Charles Mellon, but could not do much damage to the well-fortified encampment and therefore retreated into the woods.

The camp was renamed Fort Mellon in honor of the slain officer, and other forts were built between Fort Mellon and Fort Brooke in Tampa, each about a day's march from the next one. Because the Seminoles rarely attacked the forts, instead relying on guerilla-type skirmishes, the structures suffered greater deterioration from insects and forest fires. Replicas have been built of Fort Christmas east of Orlando and Fort Foster on the Hillsborough River, but only historic plaques indicate where the others stood, when known. Many such forts did not house soldiers for too long since the federal troops succeeded in either killing many of the Native Americans they encountered, capturing and sending them to Indian Territory in the West, or driving them south into the Everglades. The Seminoles, in fact, never officially signed a peace treaty with the United States, but federal officials called an end to the wars in 1858. The two hundred or so Seminoles who refused to be transported to Indian Territory in the West and who retreated to the safety of the Everglades are the direct ancestors of the approximately three thousand Seminoles who live in the state today.

After the Civil War, Fort Mellon attracted settlers, who established the small settlement of Mellonville, named after the fort. The town's name was changed to Sanford when the former U.S. minister to Belgium, Henry Sanford, bought twelve thousand acres of nearby land in 1871. Today, Sanford is the county seat of Seminole County, which had been carved out of the much larger Orange County.

Sanford, which has a population of over thirty-eight thousand, is a growing city that has become a "bedroom community" for those commuters willing to tackle I-4 to work in Orlando to the west. Sanford's airport rivals the much larger Orlando International Airport because of its ability to attract charter flights, especially from Europe.

Boaters can tie up to the public dock and walk into town, just two blocks away from the lake. A large marina is at the water's edge near the center of town; boats can be put into the water or taken out, and boaters can have their boats serviced. The downtown area is quaint and has antique shops, which attracts visitors. Officials have also built a long walkway along the river, with many places to stop and see the boats and activity along the water. Just to the north of the downtown area, but still along the waterfront, is a pair of impressive-looking buildings: the Seminole County Courthouse to the south and the Sanford City Hall to the north.

One can see all kinds of boats along the river.

Sanford is the setting for one of the most humorous episodes in the river trip that author Marjorie Kinnan Rawlings made with her friend, Dessie Smith, in 1933. As the two grubby women approached the dock at Sanford to buy some gasoline for their boat, they met the nattily dressed owner of a huge yacht who offered to have his crew drive to the nearest gas station to fill their five-gallon tins. At that point, the owner's wife, "magnificent in pink spectator sports costume," insisted that the driver take her to church instead of helping the two women. When the driver returned and got the tins filled with gasoline and the women said goodbye to the helpful yacht owner, they remarked how sad he looked at not joining them. Dessie remarked: "The poor b——. I'll bet he'd give his silk shirt to go down the river with us instead of with Pink Petticoats."

For over four decades, beginning in the 1960s, the most prominent landmarks on the northern shore of the lake were the three brightly painted smokestacks at the electric plant near I-4. Florida Power & Light dismantled them in 2003 as part of the company's ongoing conversion of the oil-fired plant to natural gas. The company's new eight power units are only 125-feet tall versus the one 300-footer and two 400-footers of the old towers. The unused power plant in Enterprise to the east of the towers is the most prominent landmark on that part of the lake.

Real estate developer Henry Shelton Sanford.

Several times a week a large tug-pushed fuel barge takes fuel from the northern part of the river to the power plant at Sanford. It carries oil today, but in the future, when the power plant switches to natural gas pumped in by a pipeline, the fuel barge may be phased out completely. The fuel barges used to run the river several times a day, but by 2004 that number was reduced to just a few times a week.

You may see the large *Rivership Romance* boat that sails out of Sanford near the Marina Hotel. The boat, which can accommodate up to two hundred passengers, has been offering popular luncheon and dinner cruises since 1982 and hearkens back to a time when steamboats plied the waters of the river to and from Sanford and Enterprise and on to Jacksonville (see chapter ten for tour information).

As in many bodies of water in Florida, fishing in Lake Monroe has declined, primarily because of a loss of aquatic habitat due to the effects of discharges from a sewage-treatment plant, the dredging of bottom sediments, and widespread exotic plant populations. Beginning in 1989, the Florida Game and Fresh Water Fish Commission, with a generous grant from the Florida Department of Environmental Regulation and its Pollution Recovery Trust Fund, revegetated the lake with native aquatic plant species. Within several years, surveyors found that such efforts enhanced sport fisheries and helped restore the lake. Even fishermen along the banks benefited from new plantings along the Sanford seawall.

The Central Florida Zoo is located near the northwestern edge of Lake Monroe just before it enters the St. Johns River. Just north of there and to the left (west), after you cross under three bridges (I-4, 19, and a railroad crossing), you will see what used to be the Port of Sanford facility, where you can dock large boats. Seeing people lounging on their tied-up boats there and receiving quizzical replies to my question ("How's the boating around here?"—"I don't know. Why would anyone want to take their boat out when they can relax at the dock?") reminded me of an observation I read somewhere: "There are boaters, and then there are boat owners."

A popular lakeside park is situated between the bridges on the north side of Lake Monroe. The dredged-out basin on the east side of the river has a small dock, restrooms, a boat-launching ramp, and an area for boaters to anchor for the night. Lake Monroe Wayside Park on the west side of the river between the bridges has a boat-launching facility and part of an old bridge extending out over the river from which you can fish. From this bridge you can see three other bridges: the I-4 bridge, the bascule bridge for the railroad, and the 17/92 bridge. This is one of the best places in Florida to see four bridges, three of which have very different designs and functions from the others. The bascule bridge is a counterbalanced drawbridge, so that when one end is lowered, the other is raised. Boaters will pass under several of these bridges on the way to Mayport.

This old bridge is one of four at the northern edge of Lake Monroe.

The oldest of the four bridges, the one that only partially extends across the river, is the Lake Monroe Bridge, built in 1932–1933 as the first electrically operated swing bridge in Florida. That structure, built with federal funds, replaced a wooden toll bridge that was manually operated. The bridge, whose construction provided economic relief for the local area—hard hit during the Depression—carried the main route that linked Daytona Beach and Tampa via DeLand, Sanford, Orlando, and Lakeland.

Just north of Lake Monroe is the town of Debary, named for Belgian Baron Frederick deBary, who came to the United States in 1840 and made a fortune importing champagne and European wines. DeBary Hall has exhibits about the history of the area (see chapter 10 for details).

Just past the zoo is an entrance to Konomac Lake. Along the south part of the lake is Fort Florida Road, which leads from Highways 15, 17, 92, and 600 west and then north to High Banks. The road commemorates Fort Florida, which used to stand on the east bank of the river, one and a half miles southwest of DeBary. General Winfield Scott selected the site for the fort/depot, which is now private property, in 1836 during the Second Seminole War.

Just past marker 99 and near 96 is the opening on the left to the Wekiva River, a waterway with ancient mounds that have enabled archaeologists to determine that people lived in the area as early as 2000 B.C. The name of the river comes from a Creek word meaning "spring of water." Nine major springs feed into the Wekiva, making it crystal clear and also one of the steepest in the state as the water falls about 1.6 feet per mile. The woods around the river are home to the largest number of Florida black bears (*Ursus americanus floridanus*), although development has reduced the number to around fifty. Black bears prefer woods full of pine trees and can sometimes be seen eating blackberries along roads. These normally shy creatures seldom attack human beings, but they can be a nuisance when they forage among garbage and campsites. One may also see rhesus monkeys *(Macaca mulatta)* in the trees, an exotic species native to Asia which, according to some, were introduced to Silver Springs for the filming of Tarzan movies in the 1920s and 1930s.

In the late 1800s, visitors could travel by steamboat to and from the St. Johns to the tiny settlement of Clay Springs near the source of the Wekiva River. The seventy-foot *Mayflower* side-wheeler with a draft of only fourteen inches used to make two trips a week between Clay Springs and Sanford. The seventeen-mile-long river, which forms the border between Seminole and Lake Counties as well as Seminole and Orange Counties, has Wekiwa (the "–wa" ending is used for the spring) Springs State Park near its source. This river is the first large tributary feeding into the St. Johns that we meet. It has benefited from the careful attention of those, such as the Friends of the Wekiva River, who want to preserve it for future generations.

In 1988, some preservationists convinced then–Republican Governor Bob Martinez to paddle a canoe down the Wekiva and see for himself what a beautiful waterway it is. He was so impressed that he joined Democratic legislators in enacting a law establishing a protective boundary of nineteen thousand acres along the river. The land inside that boundary was to remain undeveloped and the animals living there, such as the black bears and deer, were to be protected. Lake, Orange, and Seminole Counties were ordered to revamp their comprehensive plans to follow the state law. Lake and Orange Counties complied, although it took some pressure to impose a building moratorium, but Seminole County continued approving projects that seemed to violate the spirit of the new law. After the state sued Seminole County in 1999, the county finally began complying with the Wekiva Law.

The state has spent over one million dollars buying land around the Wekiva and creating a wildlife corridor that Florida black bears use between the Wekiva River Aquatic Preserve and the Ocala National Forest. Such efforts are often opposed by those who want to build more roads in Florida including a beltway around Orlando to ease some of the congestion on I-4, which links Daytona Beach, Orlando, and Tampa.

Back on the St. Johns is a dock on the east side with a sign for the City of DeBary, "The River City." Other sites along the St. Johns, such as Palatka, Green Cove Springs, or Orange Park, could probably make a stronger case for such a nickname, especially because DeBary is more on two lakes (Konomac and Monroe) than on the river, but maybe DeBary came up with the idea first.

For a very beautiful run off the river, head west just north of marker 80 and south of green marker 77. A short distance on the canal, which may have been cut by loggers taking their trees out to the river, is Hontoon Dead River, whose unfortunate name may discourage boaters from traveling on a very isolated, beautiful body of water that goes around Hontoon Island State Park. The name "dead" for this and other side waterways along the river refers more to their being dead-end ways than to any hint of pollution or putrefaction. In fact, the isolated status of such "dead" rivers provides good fishing, wonderful scenery, and a sense of what Florida used to look like a thousand years ago. In this particular "dead" river, a four to five mile stretch that comes out north of Hontoon Island, we saw more manatees and birds than on any other stretch of the St. Johns. The manatees, which swam in small groups of two or three, made their way along the river gently and slowly, diving occasionally to feed on grasses. We also saw many osprey and some hawks, and even rarer birds like the purple gallinule, which can be seen in the spring as they feed near lily pads. The most spectacular sighting was of an osprey plunging feet first into the water and catching fish that were feeding near the surface.

The relatively straight logging canals indicate how rich the area used to be for those lumbermen who cut down huge cypress trees and floated them out to the main channel and on their way north to markets. You need a boat with a relatively shallow draft to go up the canals, and a depth-marker is essential to avoid hitting fallen trees which you cannot easily see on the surface.

Blue Spring is the first major spring we meet on our way down the St. Johns. It is the largest one on the river and the only first-magnitude spring in Volusia County, pouring over one hundred million gallons of fresh water a day into the St. Johns. Scientists categorize springs according to the amount of water they produce in a certain amount of time. The flow rates are described in terms of cubic feet per second or millions of gallons per day. First-magnitude springs flow at

The Hontoon Dead River was very isolated and full of animals.

the rate of at least one hundred cubic feet per second or 64.6 million gallons per day. The United States has around seventy-five first-magnitude springs, more than one-third of which (27) are in Florida. Those first-magnitude springs pour over six billion gallons of fresh water per day into rivers and lakes.

Although the springs we encounter seem strong, the output of Blue Spring and others along the St. Johns has decreased over the last half-century because of the increasing residential and industrial use of water. The rising level of nitrates from human use of the land is also a concern to environmentalists who can gauge the changing nature of Florida's springs. The chemical essence of nitrates, which are used as fertilizers, can cause serious illnesses and even death, especially in children. These springs are one of Florida's greatest natural assets and are therefore protected by official agencies and scores of volunteers who monitor them frequently. Unlike the springs on the state's west side, which empty into the Gulf of Mexico after a relatively short run, the springs on the east side generally empty into the St. Johns, giving it increased volume, although not much more speed, as it heads north to the Atlantic Ocean.

Just south of red marker 70 is Blue Spring State Park, a very popular recreation site which attracts over three hundred thousand visitors a year. Although there is a fee for those arriving by land, those arriving by boat can enter the park without a fee (but they may not spend the night at the beach). Because the spring has a constant temperature of 72° Fahrenheit, manatees often go up the run from the colder St. Johns during winter months.

Manatees, which are also called "sea cows" or sirenians (from the sirens of Greek mythology who would lure ships onto the rocks with their mesmerizing songs), inhabit rivers, bays, canals, estuaries, and coastal areas rich in sea grass and other vegetation. These slow-moving, large hervibores can live in fresh, saline, and brackish water, preferably of a temperature above 70° Fahrenheit. Distinctive in shape, with a full middle that tapers down to a paddle-shaped tail, they eat water hyacinth and other plants and breathe through their snouts. The Florida manatee (*Trichechus manatus latirostris*), a subspecies of the West Indian manatee, averages about ten feet in length but can reach lengths of up to thirteen feet. Average adults weigh eight hundred to twelve hundred pounds, but large individuals have been known to weigh up to thirty-five hundred pounds. Females are generally larger than males. They use the two small pectoral flippers on their upper body for steering, transporting food to their mouth, and even guiding themselves along the bottom of the river.

During the colder months of the year, visitors can see manatees at Blue Spring State Park, although rangers on hand ask visitors not to swim too close to the gentle creatures, and certainly not to touch them. Day boats take visitors from Sanford down the river to see the manatees. The clarity of the water allows visitors standing on the boardwalk around the run to see them easily. All along the river you will see signs warning boaters about the occasional presence of manatees. Boaters must observe the "No Wake" zones or risk incurring a heavy fine. Even so, manatees are often wounded or killed by boat propellers. From those who survive propeller-caused gashes, rangers can sometimes identify individuals by the scars on their backs. We heard fish camp operators and some boaters complain about the "No Wake" zones, but the zones are likely to remain in place and maybe even increase as the number of manatees continues to decline. The Florida manatee is an endangered species. A January 2001 census estimated the Florida manatee population to be about 3,320. Save the Manatee Club (SMC), which former Florida Governor Bob Graham and singer/songwriter Jimmy Buffett established in 1981, is a membership-based, national nonprofit organization based in Maitland, Florida. SMC's Adopt-A-Manatee program funds public awareness and education projects, manatee research, rescue and rehabilitation efforts, and advocacy and legal actions to ensure better protection for manatees and their habitat. The organization has about forty thousand members.

The area around Blue Spring was the site of a Timucua settlement. The Timucua lived in central Florida, from the east coast to the Aucilla River, centuries before the Spanish and French arrived in the sixteenth century. The word "Timucua" probably comes from the word that the Saturiwa used for the large, varied group of tribes who inhabited much of central Florida. The Saturiwa told the French that the name of their neighbors was something that sounded like "Thimogona," which probably meant "enemy." Later, the Europeans used the derived word "Timucua" for all the Native Americans of North Florida. The Spanish and French conquered and later converted many of the Timucua to Christianity. Eventually they were exterminated through war and diseases brought by Europeans.

The large Native American mounds along and near the St. Johns testify to a large group of Native Americans living in the area for centuries. Jerald Milanich, one of the experts on Native Americans of Florida, put it this way: ". . . imagine thousands of people eating a dozen or so oysters nearly every day for a hundred generations. That would result in considerable amounts of debris, and the pre-Columbian Native Americans of east Florida dealt with it by piling their discarded shells in huge heaps near where they lived" (*Florida's Indians from Ancient Times to the Present*).

Two of the most important early white visitors to Blue Spring were the father-son team of John and William Bartram, who visited many of the sites along the river in the 1770s, during the time when Great Britain controlled Florida (1763-1783). During our trip on the St. Johns, my two boating companions and I thought of the Bartrams as our "unofficial guides" because we used their writings, especially William's.

John Bartram (1699-1777) established the first North American botanical garden in Philadelphia (1728) and became the royal botanist for King George III. As such, he was asked to go to the newly acquired Florida peninsula and explore as much of it as possible. In 1765, he took along his twenty-six-year-old son William (1739-1823), and together they named many plants previously unknown in England and its thirteen colonies in the New World. After several months of traveling through Florida, John returned to Philadelphia, but William stayed behind to try to be a planter along the St. Johns River near Picolata (see chapter six).

In 1767, William gave up farming and returned to Philadelphia, where he struggled to earn a living. In 1773, an English physician friend,

William Bartram's illustration of two alligators on the St. Johns River.

Dr. John Fothergill, paid William to head south again to collect more plant specimens and explore the Deep South. For the next four years, William traveled through the Carolinas, northern Florida, Georgia, and Alabama to the Gulf of Mexico and the Mississippi River. The Seminoles befriended him, called him "Puc Puggy" or "Flower Hunter," and helped him along the way. He would not publish his *Travels of William Bartram* until 1791, but his work in his father's botanical garden in Pennsylvania and his research attracted such luminaries as George Washington, James Madison, Alexander Hamilton, and Thomas Jefferson. More importantly, his writings made Americans and Europeans much more aware of the natural beauty and resources of Florida.

The particular edition of William Bartram's work that I prefer is *The Travels of William Bartram* (Naturalist's Edition), edited by Francis Harper (1958), because it contains the text that Bartram wrote as well as a commentary on his trips, an annotated index, maps, and photographs of the sites visited that were taken in 1939–1940. Two good commentaries about William Bartram are *Guide to William Bartram's Travels, Following the Trail of America's First Great Naturalist* by Brad Sanders and *An Outdoor Guide to Bartram's Travels* by Charles Spornick and others (see chapter ten for the complete listing).

John and William Bartram visited Blue Spring in 1766, and William returned in 1774. William's description of the spring is still relevant today: "The water is perfectly diaphanous, and here are continually a prodigious number and variety of fish; they appear as plain as though lying on a table before your eyes, although many feet deep in the water." This was the southernmost point they visited before returning down the river.

Of interest on the grounds of Blue Spring State Park is the Thursby House. Louis Thursby and his family arrived in 1856 and lived in a nearby log cabin, one of the few homesteads on the upper St. Johns before the Civil War. After the Civil War, he established one of the first steamboat landings and orange groves on the upper river. In 1872, he built a two-story frame house (the third story and kitchen of the house at the spring are not original) on a Timucuan shell mound and shipped oranges out from Orange City until harsh freezes killed the groves in the late 1800s. The restored house resembles what such a house would look like in the 1875–1887 period, when steamboats would land nearby. The cypress water tank behind the house stored rainwater collected off the roof. The family could not use the water from Blue Spring because it was too sulfurous. Visitors can learn the history of the house and of the steamboat

landing from the nearby illustrated signs, and also take tours of the house at designated times (see chapter ten for visitor information). A railroad, the Jacksonville, Tampa, and

Key West Railroad, was built in the area in 1885. It could bring visitors from Jacksonville in only four hours, versus the fourteen hours the trip would take by steamboat. The coming of the railroad ended the era of the steamboat on the St. Johns as river traffic declined.

Back on the St. Johns, boaters can venture into Lake Beresford, which the St. Johns enters for a short way before it heads west for Hontoon Island. Here, you will begin to see more houseboats than at other parts south of there because they are rented from the docks to the east of Hontoon Island. If you anchor a boat in Lake Beresford, especially a large, bulky houseboat, be aware that the thickness of the mud on the bottom can make retrieving the anchor very difficult. Boaters should pay close attention to nautical charts because the lake can be very shallow in parts. Today one can see pleasure boats and even private seaplanes using the lake. A marina on the west side of the lake rents boats and cottages and has a large boat, *Beresford Lady,* that offers cruises on the lake (see chapter ten for details about the boat.)

The town and lake of Beresford were probably named by English settlers after John Beresford, an Irish statesman during the time when the British controlled Florida (1763-1783). *Flashbacks: The Story of Central*

Florida's Past notes that during that period John and William Beresford owned twenty thousand acres near the St. Johns River and Lake Jesup, which they used to grow indigo to make a dye for the deep-blue uniforms worn by the British Navy. The Beresfords were just two of many British settlers who lived along the St. Johns during this period but who left when the Spanish retook control of Florida in 1783.

William "Billy" Bartram crossed Lake Beresford in 1774 on his way to visit Lord Beresford's plantation, which was located near present-day Beresford Station on the east side of the lake toward the north end. Because Bartram did not know how quickly Florida storms could come up in the summer, a sudden squall caught him in the lake and threatened to cause him serious harm. As it was, all the storm did was soak his papers and belongings before he could reach the safety of the Beresford Plantation. A few houses are on the north side of the lake, but there is no trace of Lord Beresford's plantation or of the place where Bartram landed.

Less than a mile down the river from Lake Beresford is Hontoon Island State Park, one of the highlights of our trip down the river.

by land from Sanford to Hontoon Island

Drivers heading west into Sanford on SR 46, then north and west on SR 415 to the east side of town, can go down Cameron Avenue to visit an ancient Native American mound after which Indian Mound Village is named. You can climb to the top of the mound on a path and see the St. Johns as it enters Lake Monroe. To reach the mound from the south, turn right off SR 415 (Celery Avenue) onto North Cameron Avenue .1 miles north of the Sanford Boat Works and Marina, then drive .1 miles to the end of the road, and turn right onto Chickasaw Drive—the mound is .1 miles on the right. A sign at the mound warns visitors not to disturb the historic site.

Celery Avenue, one of the main streets in Sanford, honors the town's most important crop in the first quarter of the twentieth century. Red Barber, who went on to a successful hall-of-fame career as a professional baseball announcer, used to pick celery in Sanford as a youngster. In those early days, the celery harvested around Sanford was so plentiful that a railroad spur to the celery fields helped planters to load it onto refrigerated freight cars and take it to northern markets. One can still see the huge former homes of the planters on Celery Avenue.

Mellonville Avenue commemorates Fort Mellon, an outpost built by federal troops during the Second Seminole War, commemorating in its name a young commander, Charles Mellon, who was killed by Seminoles there in 1837. A stone marker to the south of town at the southeast corner of North Mellonville Avenue and East Second Street notes the possible site of the fort.

The large three-story building on East First Street, which boaters can easily see from the lake, is a 1925 hotel built by Forrest Lake, an enterprising man whom local voters sent to the state legislature and then elected eleven times as mayor from 1916 to 1927. He had the state legislature establish Seminole County out of the much larger Orange County and built the Forrest Lake Hotel to cater to the hordes of visitors who were expected to visit the pretty town on Lake Monroe, but the real estate crash put him and the town into deep debt. He was eventually sent to state prison for three years for financial misdeeds and returned to Sanford, where he died in 1939, penniless and hated. The city bought the hotel and renamed it the Mayfair Inn. After World War II, the city leased it to the New York Giants baseball team, which had spring training in Sanford before moving to the west coast. Eventually, the New Tribes Mission, a nondenominational, evangelical organization, took over the structure and turned it into its national headquarters.

To the immediate west of the New Tribes Mission building is the Sanford Museum at 520 E. First Street, where visitors can see artifacts and documents about the history of the area.

About five miles south of Sanford on SR 427 near Longwood is Big Tree County Park, which contains a 3,500-year-old bald cypress tree. The eleven-story-tall tree, which can be seen from the St. Johns, is called "The Senator" after a state senator, M.O. Overstreet, who donated the tree and surrounding land to the county in 1951. The tree is one of the few survivors of thousands of ancient trees that existed in Florida before loggers felled them. President Calvin Coolidge dedicated the tree to the public in 1929, after which the Works Projects Administration built the first walkway over the swamp there.

Drivers can head around the eastern and northern edge of Lake Monroe by going on Highway 415 east of town and then turning left on Reed Ellis Road to Enterprise-Osteen Road around Lake Bethel. A road to the left of Enterprise Osteen will take you to Stone Island, which is on the lake. When the Bartrams (John and his son William) camped there in 1765 as they made their way through Florida, they could see the burial mounds that generations of Native Americans had built. Today, Stone Island has private roads that prevent visitors from visiting the older sites, especially along the lake.

Farther west on Enterprise-Osteen Road is the site of Enterprise, once the seat of Volusia County when it was created by the Florida Legislature in 1854, but now the site of a power plant. A New Englander named Jacob Brock, who bought the *Darlington* steamboat in 1853 and moved down with his children, developed Enterprise. Realizing that the St. Johns would be the water highway for new settlers heading south, he settled on the north side of Lake Monroe, built a hotel and then a dock into the lake, and began entertaining guests. The Brock Hotel existed into the 1930s, but railroads reduced traffic on the waterway, and the hotel was eventually torn down. Much of its timber was used in nearby houses. The hotel stood where the United Methodist Children's Home stands today.

Very little remains of the former town. A double row of pilings in the lake is about the only remnant of the once-busy dock where steamboats used to stop on their way to and from ports to the north. The huge house that Frederick deBary built in Enterprise in 1871 is now in the city limits of DeBary, a relatively new city established in 1993. The eastern part of Enterprise was taken over by the development of Deltona in the mid-1960s. That settlement did not become a city until 1995.

The city of DeBary near Lake Monroe is worth visiting by car, especially for DeBary Hall, a large mansion built in 1871 by Frederick deBary, a Belgian baron who imported champagne and European wines. Distinguished guests to DeBary Hall included Presidents Ulysses Grant and Grover Cleveland, General William Tecumseh Sherman, and even the Prince of Wales.

After visiting the Hall, go west on Dirksen Drive, a two-lane road that skirts the DeBary Bayou, a swamp with cabbage palms and deciduous trees that used to host many deer, panthers, and black bears. Dirksen Drive leads to Mansion Boulevard and to a former dock that steamboats used in the second half of the nineteenth century to take cargo and passengers along the St. Johns. Horse-drawn carriages would take arriving passengers from the river to DeBary Hall.

At 37 Dirksen Drive is Gemini Springs County Park, about a quarter-mile west of DeBary Hall. Formerly the site of a sugar plantation, the park now has a fishing area fed by two freshwater springs, thus its name Gemini.

A path winds around the park for three-quarters of a mile and allows visitors to see an unspoiled landscape that probably has not changed in hundreds of years. Boaters can rent canoes there. Only very shallow draft boats can make it to and from Lake Monroe.

Gemini Springs County Park is very large and has many amenities.

Drivers continuing west on Enterprise Road can go across the busy US 17/92 Highway, then turn left on Shell Road, which will lead to Fort Florida Road. The road, which was named for a depot built during the Second Seminole War and situated on the east bank of the St. Johns (but which is now on private property), leads around Konomac Lake, but developments along the river prevent easy access to the St. Johns. The road eventually comes out at High Banks Road, which leads to the river, a boat launch, restaurant, and trailer park (see chapter 10 for details).

To continue north, go back to Highways 17/92 and head north to Orange City, where a road to the west leads to Blue Spring State Park.

3 Hontoon Island through Astor

"Penny hallooed on the west side of the river to call the ferry from the east. The sound echoed down the river. A boy appeared on the opposite bank. He came leisurely. For an instant it seemed to Jody that the boy had an enviable life, pulling the ferry back and forth across the river. Then it occurred to him that such a life was quite without freedom. There would be for such a boy no hunts, no jaunts into the scrub, no Flag. He was glad he was not the ferryman's son."

—*Marjorie Kinnan Rawlings,* The Yearling

by water from Hontoon Island through Astor

Hontoon Island State Park on the western side of the St. Johns is one of the most significant historic sites on the whole river. Formerly occupied by the Timucuans five to six thousand years ago, the island has two large mounds formed from the discarded shells of snails gathered from the river. A replica of a large owl totem, the original of which was found in 1955, stands in the picnic area; the original is at Fort Caroline National Park above Jacksonville (see chapter nine). The owl totem, found in the wood-preserving muck during the excavation of the marina across the way, is one of the largest wooden carvings ever found in Florida and the only such totem found on the east coast of the United States.

The two mounds are full of empty snail shells. A sign at one of the mounds warns visitors not to take anything from the area. Nowadays snails are a vector for a nasty parasite, so one wonders whether the Native Americans cooked their snails until they were very well done or had severe stomach problems. One writer suggested that the face on the owl totem looks like it had a terrible bellyache!

As I stood on the edge of the state park, the ranger pointed across the river to the houses and boat docks and told me that the banks used to be lined with shell mounds, a testament to the thousands of Native Americans who used to live along the St. Johns in countless villages. In the 1930s, long before archaeologists made the public aware of how valuable such shell mounds are for understanding past

A replica of the owl totem is near the ferry landing on the island.

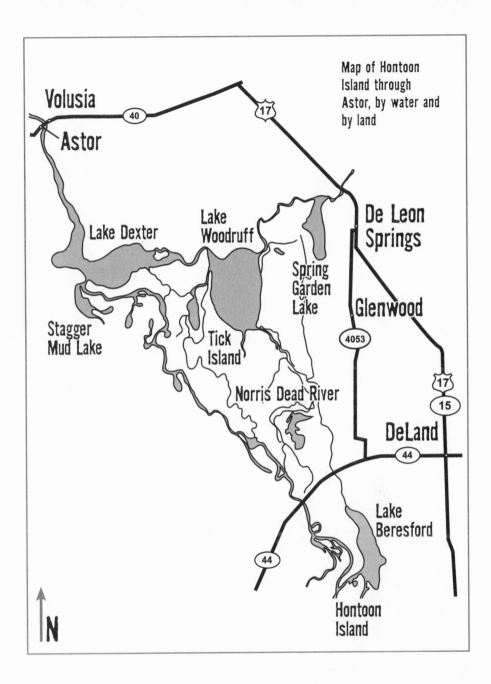

Volusia

Astor

40

17

Map of Hontoon
Island through
Astor, by water and
by land

Lake Dexter

Lake
Woodruff

De Leon
Springs

Spring
Garden
Lake

Glenwood

Stagger
Mud Lake

Tick
Island

4053

Norris Dead River

17

15

DeLand

44

Lake
Beresford

44

N

Hontoon
Island

Native American cultures, workers trucked away huge amounts of these middens with heavy machinery in order to make road beds throughout the state.

Long after the Native Americans were driven out, settlers moved onto Hontoon Island to fish, farm, and raise cattle. They also used it as a boatyard, a fish-packing house, a pioneer homestead, and a cattle ranch. In 1967, the state bought the island, which is about three miles long and one mile wide, and made it into a state park.

If the rangers are not too busy, they may show visitors some of the albums of photographs taken on the island of flora, fauna, and historic sites. A museum behind the ranger station gives a history of the area, including some of the animals one can find on the island. The Peabody Museum at Harvard University has some of the archaeological artifacts found on the island.

A self-guided trail beginning at the Ranger Station goes along Hontoon Dead River to a large mound at the southwest corner of the island; it takes one to two hours to make the round-trip walk. Be aware that the path is primitive, the signs are very few, wildlife roams the island (a pygmy rattlesnake blocked my path near the shell mound), and walkers can easily get lost if they wander off the path, as I did (see chapter ten for visiting information).

Of particular interest to birdwatchers are the songbirds and woodpeckers in the hammocks on either side of the path. The scrubby flatwoods in the interior of the island have warblers and vireos. One of the very few small

Parts of the island have ponds full of lily pads.

signs along the way pointed out the sabal palm, also called the cabbage palm. Florida's official state tree used to be fashioned by Native Americans and early white pioneers into log houses. The Seminoles still use the leaves today for the roofs of their chickees. The heart of the tree, called swamp cabbage, is a delicacy in a few restaurants around the state, but taking that part of the tree will kill it.

Signs along the river, this one across from Hontoon Island, mention William Bartram's famous trip.

Back at the University of Florida, I spoke with Dr. Kenneth Sassaman, a professor of anthropology and archaeology who led archaeological field schools on Hontoon Island and at the Thursby House near Blue Spring farther south. He pointed out that such fieldwork, besides protecting archaeological resources in the state, also increases our knowledge of the Native Americans who lived there thousands of years ago. He and his students found, for example, that—despite the extensive shell mining done there by road-building companies—subsurface middens still exist and await further archaeological digging that would tell us more about our ancestors.

As my two boating companions and I headed north on the river, we saw more houseboats than at any other place, partly because of the rental facilities across from Hontoon Island. Having rented such a boat several years before, I knew how difficult they are to handle and that

This section of the river had more houseboats than any other.

other boaters need to keep a wide berth. A quick lesson in how to manage houseboats: at first they are quite difficult to handle since they respond very slowly to a turn of the steering wheel; after some practice, however, they are fun to use. The secret is to think ahead ten minutes or so. Because the single propeller responds very slowly, sometimes as much as thirty seconds or more after the pilot turns the driving wheel, a panicky pilot may at first spin the wheel all the way over in one direction, only to find the hulky boat not responding for a half-minute. And then, because the pilot has spun the wheel to one extreme, the boat tends to go back and forth with the jerky motions of the pilot.

About three miles north of Hontoon Island State Park is the White-hair Bridge, which takes SR 44 across the river. Although the St. Johns has several ferries that cross it, most travelers use the bridges to get from one side to the other. Just north of that bridge at red marker 38, boaters with shallow-draft boats can take a side trip to DeLeon Springs by way of Norris Dead River. After almost five miles of winding turns, visitors will come to a sign leading off to Highland Park Fish Camp/Marina. The distance from there to Lake Woodruff is a little over three miles, then another 4.5 miles to DeLeon Springs State Recreation Area, which has swimming, a boat ramp, boat rentals, food, ice, water, and toilets.

The springs are named after Juan Ponce de León, who supposedly stopped there on his trek to find the Fountain of Youth in the 1500s. I know that the story is apocryphal, that Ponce de León did not venture much into the interior of Florida, but the name is one that conjures up a link to the Spanish past and to a hope that many visitors to Florida have had over the years to find their "youth" again. When I visited the Fountain of Youth park in St. Augustine and drank from the "youth-instilling" waters sold there, I thought back to the stories of Ponce de León and how the Native Americans probably used such myths to send the Spanish on their way: "Oh, you want to find the Fountain of Youth. We know where it is. It's actually quite a ways from here, over the next river (or lake or hill). That's where'll you find it, but definitely not around here." Ponce de León, in fact, was probably more interested in finding gold than he was in any elixir or water.

And yet, in *Ponce de León's Fountain of Youth: History of a Geographical Myth* by Leonardo Olschki, it is said that the search for the Fountain of Youth may in fact go back to the belief by Columbus and his companion/successor, Ponce de León, that they had discovered Asia in the 1490s, and that therefore they might find some of the wonders and marvels, like a Fountain of Youth, long associated with that continent.

Nineteenth-century promotions for Florida claimed that DeLeon Springs were "impregnated with a deliciously healthy combination of soda and sulphur." The springs, which have a dam that forms a popular swimming and picnic area, pump twenty million gallons of fresh water a day, most of which finds itself into the St. Johns by way of Spring Garden Lake, Lake Woodruff, and Lake Dexter. Hydrologists rate DeLeon Springs as a second-magnitude artesian vent, meaning it has an average flow rate of between ten and one hundred cubic feet per second. Seventy of Florida's springs are in this category.

Colonel Orlando Rees installed the large waterwheel, which seems to be in good shape, in order to grind sugar cane. Then the site came under attack by Seminoles during the Second Seminole War (1835–1842). During the Civil War, locals used the waterwheel to produce corn meal and sugar for the Rebels. When Union troops captured the area, they destroyed many of the facilities to ensure that the Confederates would not be able to use the grinding material.

Springs such as DeLeon helped attract new settlers to Central Florida in the nineteenth century, just as they have since 5000 B.C. The navigable streams and rivers formed from the outpouring of the springs allowed movement from place to place as well as a good source of fish for consumption.

The place became a resort in the 1880s and attracted many health-seekers with its pleasant 72° water temperature all year-round. Boaters can launch canoes and kayaks, which they can rent there too, and paddle around Spring Garden Lake and Lake Woodruff National Wildlife Refuge.

When my boating companions and I visited the park, we had to take refuge in the picnic pavilion from a very severe thunderstorm with flashing lightning and a torrential downpour. We knew the summer storm would quickly pass, as it soon did, but such storms always surprise first-time visitors to Florida during the summer.

Heading back to the St. Johns, boaters pass through the shallow Spring Garden Creek, through the Lake Woodruff National Wildlife Refuge, and into the 2,200–acre Lake Woodruff. Established in 1964, the refuge attracts endangered and threatened species such as the alligator, the bald eagle, gopher tortoise, indigo snake, limpkin, manatee, snail kite, and wood stork. The gopher tortoise digs burrows in the sandy soil, thus providing homes for frogs, mammals, and snakes. The indigo snake, a threatened species in Florida, is the largest non-venomous snake in North America. We heard many limpkins along the way and saw quite a few of the large, slow–moving birds in the swamps as they sought out freshwater snails on the stems of plants. The snail kite, formerly called the Everglades kite, is a tropical bird that feeds on the apple snail found in the grasses of the wetlands. The wood stork, also known as the wood ibis, ironhead, and flinthead, is the only stork in this country.

The wildlife refuge consists of a freshwater marsh (11,100 acres), hardwood swamp (4,800 acres), upland (3,400 acres), as well as lakes, streams, and canals (1,000 acres). Over thirty thousand people visit the refuge each year, primarily to observe the wildlife from designated posts and also to fish. Spring Garden Creek is one of the best places on the whole river to see many species of birds.

The establishment of wildlife refuges like the one on Lake Woodruff and the purchase of lands along the St. Johns and other Florida rivers by conservation groups and state/federal agencies has helped to some degree in preserving and restoring such rivers. Whereas in the eighteenth and nineteenth centuries officials spent much time, energy, and money buying up and draining marshes for the development of farms and towns, that idea changed dramatically in the late twentieth and early twenty-first centuries.

After decades of so-called flood-control projects, some of which led to increased dangers from wildfires that were not stopped by marshes, officials involved with the St. Johns emphasize preservation and resto-ration of plant and animal resources. Scientists writing in *Ecosystems of*

Florida, edited by Ronald Myers and John Ewel, note that "the historic importance of the surrounding marshes in maintaining the quality of the deeper water habitats is now recognized." State and federal governments have been purchasing and restoring marshes along the river as well as developing water conservation areas.

The bad news is that drained marshes can never be totally restored to their primitive condition. The good news is that scientists working with the St. Johns River Water Management District and overseeing organizations like the St. Johns Riverkeepers hold periodic cleanups of the river, monitor changes proposed by governmental agencies along the river, and keep tabs on pollution.

America's greatest ornithologist of the nineteenth century, John James Audubon, went, by a small boat, from Spring Garden Creek into Lake Woodruff and then Lake Dexter to the St. Johns in 1832. On his trips through Florida, including along the St. Johns, Audubon shot and killed birds and alligators in order to examine them closely and make his drawings as accurate as possible. An entry in his journal reads: "One morning we saw a monstrous fellow lying on the shore. I was desirous of obtaining him to make an accurate drawing of his head, and, accompanied by my assistant and two of the sailors, proceeded cautiously towards him. When within a few yards, one of us fired, and sent through his side an ounce ball, which tore open a hole large enough to receive a man's hand." Today, of course, ornithologists do not kill birds to sketch or draw them more accurately, but customs were different in Audubon's time.

Atlantic stingrays make their home in the Spring Garden Creek/Run, a place associated with the St. Johns. Although edible, the stingrays, which are the only freshwater stingrays in North America, have sharp barbs that can cause extreme pain. People wading in water that has the stingrays shuffle their feet in order to scare them away. Careful waders may notice lumpy pancake shapes along the flat bottom of the river with their long, whiplike tails extending outward. Fishermen using live bait in the river have reported easily catching a dozen or so of the rays, but the fish, other than for their "wings," which make good filets, are not worth the trouble of catching. Their long stingers contain a toxin that causes intense pain to those unlucky enough to step on one, and they also have a substance that will kill the tissue near the wound. Those unfortunate enough to encounter one will long remember the unpleasant experience.

After leaving Lake Woodruff, we passed to the south of Tick Island, an important site for archaeologists examining the Native American presence in Florida. Tick Island has middens or mounds made up of the many shells discarded by Native Americans many years ago; one of them was used as a burial place for as many as 175 corpses. In one of the best books on the subject, *Florida Indians and the Invasion from Europe,* author Jerald Milanich points out that such shell mounds are associated with the period from 5000 B.C.–3000 B.C. By then, Native Americans had already been living in Florida for seven thousand years.

During this period, the climate became milder in Florida, and the filling of the lakes and rivers allowed them to live in many places throughout the peninsula and not just around springs, as they had done in the previous ages. Another major change was that many of them were living in settlements, for example along lakes and rivers like Lake Woodruff, rather than constantly moving around in search of large animals to hunt. The change may have been due to the extinction of those animals and to the increasingly widespread practice of hunting smaller animals, cultivating crops, and eating shellfish.

In the midden that was a burial site, the Native Americans had dug a large hole and buried the corpses; then they covered over the midden and sealed it with dirt, probably to keep out animals. Workers destroyed much of the archaeological evidence in the 1950s when they took away the shells and dirt by barge to a machine that resembled a large washing machine near DeLeon Springs which used pressurized water to remove the sand and dirt from the fill. Workers first sold the washed shell for use in the drainage fields of septic tank systems, and then sold the sand and dirt washed from the shells for use in driveways and fill. Such ravaging of the Native American site at Tick Island is no longer allowed because the island is part of Lake Woodruff National Wildlife Refuge.

The isolation of Tick Island, surrounded by swamp and far from the usual path of boaters, may allow it to stay relatively undisturbed, except by archaeologists trying to learn more about our past. Imaginative boaters/visitors can picture what life must have been like on this island, which rises ten to eighteen feet above the swamp. The people there might even have carved a totem similar to the one erected at Hontoon Island.

The flow from DeLeon Springs, which—as a second-magnitude spring—averages between six million and sixty-four million gallons a day, makes its way through Lake Woodruff and then Lake Dexter to the St. Johns. Just southwest of Lake Dexter is Stagger Mud Lake, which the St. Johns skirts on the northern edge as the river passes between Lake Dexter and Stagger Mud Lake. The point of land to the left, Idlewilde Point, is where William Bartram had his famous encounter with the alligators as he attempted to make his way across the water to a distant shore. This is what Bartram wrote:

Not thinking it prudent to take my fusee [a large-headed friction match that can burn in a wind] with me, lest I might lose it overboard in case of a battle, which I had every reason to dread before my return, I therefore furnished myself with a club for my defence, went on board [his small canoe], and penetrating the first line of those [alligators] which surrounded my harbour, they gave way; but being pursued by several very large ones, I kept strictly on the watch, and paddled with all my might towards the entrance of the lagoon, hoping to be sheltered there from the multitude of my assailants; but ere I had halfway reached the place, I was attacked on all sides, several endeavouring to overset the canoe. My situation now became precarious to the last degree: two very large ones attacked me closely, at the same instant, rushing up with their heads and part of their bodies above the water, roaring terribly and belching floods of water over me. They struck their jaws together so close to my ears, as almost to stun me, and I expected every moment to be dragged out of the boat and instantly devoured, but I applied my weapons so effectually about me, though at random, that I was so successful as to beat them off a little; when, finding that they designed to renew the battle, I made for the shore, as the only means left me for my preservation, for, by keeping close to it, I should have my enemies on one side of me only, whereas I was before surrounded by them, and there was a probability, if pushed to

We saw a lonely alligator near where Bartram saw hundreds.

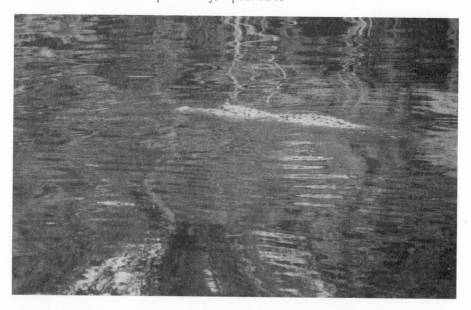

the last extremity, of saving myself, by jumping out of the canoe on shore, as it is easy to outwalk them on land, although comparatively as swift as lightning in the water.

This selection, which is on pages 119–120 of his *Travels,* comes right before Bartram's astonishment at seeing a huge number of alligators "in such incredible numbers, and so close together from shore to shore, that it would have been easy to have walked across on their heads, had the animals been harmless."

Even if we give Bartram some hyperbolic license, travelers in Florida today will not see such large numbers of alligators in one, natural place, and the animals, which he described as reaching twenty feet in length, are not nearly as long. Years of being hunted, to the point that they were declared a threatened, endangered species, have resulted in far fewer gators today and most of them being much smaller than in the eighteenth century, when Bartram visited.

We saw alligators along the upper (southern) parts of the river, but they avoided us as much as possible. When I airboated toward the start of the river, I saw very few alligators, but I went during hunting season, when the gators were fair game to those with licenses. Because of encroaching development on much of the river, we tended to see the gators on side rivers or on very isolated banks, usually alone and never in groups of more than a few.

It took a long time for Floridians, some of whom killed hundreds and hundreds of gators for shoes and bags, to realize how important alligators are for the well-being of swamps. They form so-called "alligator holes" during dry periods, inside of which water collects and fish and other creatures can live. Gators court in May with a violence on the part of the males that may frighten sightseers. But, for the most part, the reptiles want to stay by themselves, far away from mankind if possible.

If you go straight north from Whitehair Bridge and do not take the side trip to DeLeon Springs, you have a very pretty, relatively uninhabited section bordered on both sides by swamp. Harris Creek meanders along the east side of the St. Johns and joins the water coming from Lake Woodruff.

To the southwest of Lake Woodruff on the west bank of the river is the former site of St. Francis, also formerly known as Old Town. The pilings in the water there hearken back to a time when a hotel stood along the river. L.H. Harris, a doctor from Pittsburgh, Pennsylvania, bought a large tract of land along the river from James Owens Sr., and founded St. Francis in 1887. The town had a weekly newspaper (*The Florida Facts*), a post office, general store, hotel, and warehouse, as well as wharves, many homes, and several hundred acres of citrus trees. The town flourished until the Big Freeze of 1894–1895, when many residents abandoned the place. St. Francis Dead River leads off to the south, an isolated river that few people travel.

When we pass Dexter's Point on the eastern shore, we have about a two-mile, straight run up to Astor. Houses dot the shore, especially on the western part, where canals shoot off the river and make for expensive "waterfront" homes, even though they are not on the river. Although we do not see a sign, we know the place is Astor. It is one of the places along the river that once had lofty ambitions and might have become a much larger town if circumstances had helped more. The town used to be called Fort Butler, for a Colonel Robert Butler of the 4th Infantry during the Second Seminole War.

In 1763, at the start of the British occupation of Florida, trader James Spalding established his upper store where Astor is today. He chose the spot because that was where three Native-American trails crossed and where the Native Americans launched their canoes for fishing and hunting. The Bartrams (John and William) visited the trading post in 1765, and William returned nine years later alone. The store would later become part of the Panton & Leslie trading empire and would be moved to the east side of the river, where Volusia is today.

In 1838, Captain E.S. Winder and his soldiers built the fort, which consisted of a log stockade and barracks for the garrison, whose duty it was to protect the river, an important communication artery with garrisons in central Florida. Captain Winder and his troops abandoned the fort in 1839, and his troops marched against the Native Americans. Union troops occupied the fort during the Civil War until Confederate Captain J.J. Dickison and his troops captured it in 1864, taking 88 infantry and 6 cavalry prisoners. (More about Captain Dickison later.)

In 1874, William Astor, grandson of self-made millionaire John Jacob Astor I, bought almost thirteen thousand acres of land near present-day Astor, laid out a town of twelve thousand acres, and named it Manhattan. Nearby Lake Schermerhorn was named after William Astor's wife, Caroline Schermerhorn Astor. William Astor built a railroad from Astor Landing to Lake Eustis and joined it there with the Central Florida Railroad, forming the St. Johns, Lake Eustis and Gulf Railroad Company.

The town began to prosper, hotels were built, stores were opened, and more and more people moved in.

When William Astor died, his son, John Jacob Astor IV, inherited the estate, but a freeze halted the prosperity of the settlement, and then the death of John Jacob Astor IV in the *Titanic* disaster and the lack of interest in the settlement by Astor's son, William Vincent Astor, led to its demise, especially after some of the buildings burned down and the railroad made steamboat traffic on the St. Johns less desirable. Today, Astor is a small town with a wonderful location and the potential for once again growing as more and more people discover its charms.

The town on the eastern shore, Volusia, is connected to Astor by the drawbridge on SR 40. Before the drawbridge was built, there had been a ferry from Volusia to Astor, as Marjorie Kinnan Rawlings described in *The Yearling*. The little town of Volusia, which actually gave its name to the large county that also has three large beach towns (Daytona, Ormond, and New Smyrna Beach), may have taken its name from a Native American word or may have been the pronunciation of the name of a Belgian or Frenchman named Veluche (pronounced "vooLOOshay") who had a trading post at the landing on the river during the British occupation of the territory (1763–1783).

The building of a drawbridge over the river in 1926 brought Astor and Volusia closer and facilitated transportation to the east coast, for example Daytona and Ormond Beach. The first bridge tender, McQueen Johnson, was killed on the bridge by an unknown assailant that same year, but his death was never fully investigated because of a fluke: when he fell dead in the middle of the bridge, his head landed in Lake County, but the rest of his body was in Volusia County, and so both counties refused to claim jurisdiction.

The house at 1968 Alice Drive just north of the bridge on the Volusia side is where Barney Dillard (1864–1962) lived and where he hosted author Marjorie Kinnan Rawlings in the 1930s and told her many of the stories she used in *The Yearling*. The live oak near the bridge has a marker declaring it a historic site, as well as a sign indicating that the Pierson Garden Club placed a Bartram Trail marker there. Local residents call the tree the Volusia Oak or Dillard Oak.

North of Astor is where the St. Johns apparently used to curve treacherously around Morrison Island until engineers blasted out the neck of the island to make the river much straighter and therefore more maneuverable for large ships like the fuel barge that goes to and from Sanford.

To reach Hontoon Island State Park from DeLand, take SR 44 west past Spring Garden Avenue (CR 15A) and follow the signs to Old New York Avenue and the parking lot next to the river. The free ferry crosses to and from the state park throughout the day.

Those traveling by land can go east on SR 44 at Whitehair Bridge, then north on Grand Avenue (CR 4053) to Ponce de Leon Springs to the east of Lake Woodruff. Highway 17/15 can take you north to SR 40, which goes between Ormond Beach on the east coast to Astor and Volusia, then Ocala to the west. On the western side of the St. Johns small roads branch off of SR 40, but the river, which serves as the border between Lake and Volusia Counties, has many swamps along its western bank.

One favorite spot in the Ocala National Forest is Alexander Springs, which eventually reaches the St. Johns. The springs are north of SR 445, which branches to the east of SR 19. Alexander Springs, which flows into the seven-mile-long Alexander Creek, is a first-magnitude spring and, as part of the Ocala National Forest, has the largest flow of any natural spring on U.S. government land.

4

Lake George
to
Fruitland

"A spring as clear as well water

bubbled up from nowhere in the

sand. It was as though the banks

cupped green leafy hands to hold

it. There was a whirlpool where the

water rose from the earth. Grains of

sand boiled in it."

—*Marjorie Kinnan Rawlings,* The Yearling

by water from Lake George to Fruitland

Marjorie Kinnan Rawlings was one of many who have used the setting and specific experiences of the St. Johns River in their writings. William Bartram and his father, John, were two of the earliest white visitors to the St. Johns when they traveled up the river in 1765, two years after the British took control of Florida. The *Dictionary of American Biography* calls the father, John (1699–1777), "the first native American botanist" because of his pioneering work in collecting many seeds and plants from the east coast of the thirteen American colonies, for which the British named him the "Royal Botanist." The Bartrams, Quakers from Pennsylvania, traveled as far as Lake Harney up the St. Johns and were probably the first Europeans to venture so far up the river.

William returned alone in 1774 to explore much of the river, meet with Native Americans, make detailed notes about the flora and fauna he encountered, and describe a Florida that would be gone in another hundred years. To this day, his *Travels through North and South Carolina, Georgia, and East and West Florida* (1791) is a classic for its details about a land that has long gone.

When my two boating companions and I left Volusia early in the morning, we headed down the river to the great expanse of Lake George, the second-largest natural freshwater lake in Florida. At seventy-two square miles, it stretches six miles wide and twelve miles long, and drains 3,600 square miles. Its 46,000 acres makes it second to Lake Okeechobee to the south. The name, which commemorates King George III, dates from the two decades (1763–1783) when the British occupied east Florida. The Spanish called Lake George the Lake of San Antonio, possibly because the Franciscan mission at Mount Royal on the northern edge of the lake was called San Antonio de Enacape.

The lake can be very rough to boat on, especially during a strong wind or any kind of storm. Some boaters have been known to go behind one of the slowly-moving tugs that carry fuel up and down the river—although they do move slowly, they break up any waves on the lake and offer some protection from the wind. The turbulence from the tug props prevents waves from quickly forming behind the towed barge.

The Ocala National Forest borders the western side of the lake, while the eastern side is mostly swampy, and the southern side borders Lake George State Forest. Although mostly uninhabited around its shores, Lake

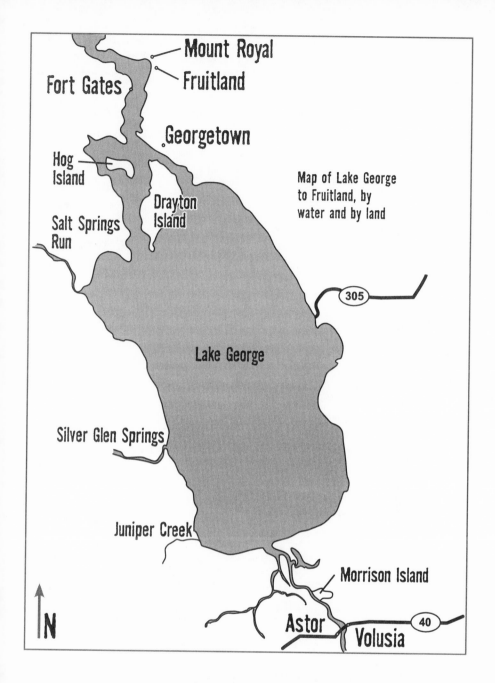

Map of Lake George to Fruitland, by water and by land

George has on its western side three of the most popular springs in the state: Juniper, Silver Glen, and Salt Springs. Wildlife teems all around the lake and its borders. Scientists have recorded seeing white-tailed deer, turkeys, the endangered red-cockaded woodpecker, sandhill cranes, and

American kestrels. The latter are small hawks that feed on deer mice, voles, lizards, frogs, and small snakes. While a small group of sandhill cranes make their permanent home to the west of Lake George, a much larger number stop there during the colder winter months.

It has, in fact, the largest breeding population of bald eagles in the lower 48 states. At the southern entrance to Lake George, the Volusia Bar Lighthouse used to mark the river entrance. The two-story wooden house on stilts had a light on the top as well as a fog horn. Even after the light was removed in the early part of the twentieth century, the person stationed there maintained kerosene lanterns on the channel markers.

A tragic incident involving the lighthouse was the unsolved homicide in 1938 of the man who tended the light, A.J. Anderson. He died from a broken neck, a mystery which has never been solved. After the U.S. government abandoned the lighthouse in the 1940s, squatters, campers, and fishermen used it to escape from the sudden storms that arise on the lake. The deteriorating structure finally burned in the early 1970s, but a few remnants can still be seen there.

The water is so shallow near the southern part of the lake that a series of markers, including a rear-range marker, and a two-sided wooden, long channel marker assist the pilots of boats and larger ships, such as the fuel barge on its way to and from Sanford. Off the western edge of the wooden channel markers that mark the treacherous and shallow Volusia Bar is a sunken three-master that can clearly be seen. The

Volusia Bar Lighthouse
(circa 1930)

wooden fencelike structure of the channel marker sometimes houses osprey nests, which are far away from predators and therefore relatively safe. William Bartram described Lake George in 1773 as "the little ocean" that dwarfed his boat: "My vessel at once diminished to a nut-shell on the swelling seas, and at the distance of a few miles, must appear to the surprised observer as some aquatic animal, at intervals emerging from its surface."

During World War II, thousands of airmen trained up and down the river and dropped their bombs on Lake George in preparation for going overseas to combat. Among the air bases in the vicinity was the DeLand Naval Air Station. During the war, the U.S. Navy trained young men in bombing and gunnery for three months at a time. Navigation charts still indicate a bombing range on the eastern half of the lake, but the "bombs" dropped are actually smoke markers that a spotter in a tower on the shore scores as to their accuracy. The purpose is to train the pilots in marksmanship, not in blowing up fish. More usually, Navy planes, often from the Jacksonville Naval Air Station, drop bombs on the Pinecastle bombing range in the Ocala National Forest. Pinecastle, in fact, is the only Navy bombing range on the East coast where live ordnance can be used.

As Marjorie Kinnan Rawlings did in her 1933 trip down the river, we chose to cross Lake George in the morning, especially because sudden afternoon summer storms can wreak havoc on a small boat in the middle of the huge lake. Unlike Rawlings and her companion, who headed away from the comfort of the west shore (and paid the price when they hit whitecaps and a turbulent lake), we stayed close to shore. While most of the settlements and springs are on the western shore of the lake, the eastern shore has two: Deadman's Landing and Pine Island Resort (see chapter 10 for details). The western shore has three springs that can be reached by boat or land: Juniper, Silver Glen, and Salt, all of which are very busy on the weekends, especially in warm weather.

The first such spring, Juniper, is west-northwest of the southern entrance to Lake George and up Juniper Creek. The Juniper Springs Recreation Area up the creek is a favorite swimming area for visitors, and boaters can launch their canoes below the Mill House. One can see so-called "sand boils" in the creek leading up to the springs. The cool water coming up from the Floridan aquifer pushes sand out, as described in this chapter's opening quotation.

The Civilian Conservation Corps (CCC) built the pool and the millhouse there in 1935 as part of the program which put thousands of Americans

to work on projects around the country. The millhouse, which still turns today to show visitors what it would have looked like in its heyday, generated electrical power for the campground. Eight million gallons of fresh water each day turned the waterwheel, which operated the electrical system inside the millhouse. The building next to the working waterwheel has served as living quarters for the concessioner who worked there, a workshop for a wildlife biologist, and a visitor information center, which is what it is today.

Fern Hammock Spring, which is several miles west of the pool, joins Juniper Spring to produce about twenty million gallons of fresh water each day. Boaters can launch their boats at SR 19 on the southwest side of the bridge. Swimmers, tubers, and snorkelers are not allowed on the run, only boaters. The last part of the run, as it enters Lake George, is very wide, but very shallow, which makes it difficult for boats to maneuver.

Many alligators swim in the area between the swimming area of the park and the lake. That became painfully clear in September 1997, when an eleven-foot, eight-inch-long, 450-pound bull alligator attacked a swimmer in the waters of Juniper Run, about a mile upstream from Juniper Springs. The man, who had been canoeing but was swimming in the early evening, swam too close to the gator, which attacked the man, held the man's head in his powerful jaws, and shook him a few times before letting him go. Park rangers concluded that the gator, which could have easily crushed the man's head in its powerful jaws, was simply warning him from snorkeling in the gator's territory. Rangers point out that alligators are most active early in the afternoon and late in the afternoon.

The next spring along the western shore as we head north is Silver Glen Springs, a first-magnitude spring about two miles north of the entrance to Juniper Creek. The entrance to each of the springs is difficult to see from afar, and boaters have to beware of the shallow water on either side of the entrances. The clarity of the water, especially as boaters go toward the spring head, allows one to see the mullet and blue tilapia that swim there. Snorkelers may see hundreds of fish, especially striped bass, as if they were stacked on top of each other around the spring holes, especially during the warm months, when they seek out the coolness of the 72° water.

Of particular concern to environmentalists is the intrusive blue tilapia (*Tilapia aurea*), which was introduced into phosphate mining pits in Hillsborough County near the west coast of Florida in 1961 and somehow made its way this far. Scientists had hoped that the fish would be a noncompetitive, catchable sportfish that could also be used as a plant-eater to control some of the many exotic grasses in the waterways. The experiment finally showed that the fish would be detrimental in Florida waters, but somehow someone took some of the tilapia and stocked it in ponds and public lakes. Seven years later, the fish is becoming one of the fastest-spreading exotics in the state. Sometimes mistakenly referred to as "Nile bream" or "Nile perch," the foot-long fish has become very unwelcome as it overwhelms native species such as the bass. Some areas in bodies of fresh water with dense tilapia populations are nearly devoid of vegetation and native fish.

Silver Glen National Forest Recreation Area, which contains the springs, used to be a large private campground but has slowly been changed into more of a wilderness environment. As such, only swimming and snorkeling are permitted. Scuba diving and fishing in the "boil" area are not permitted. At the eastern edge of the entrance to Silver Glen Springs is the privately owned Juniper Club, which dates back to 1909, when a group of hunters from Louisville, Kentucky, bought a large tract of land there. In the large, private clubhouse at the entrance to the river, the Junipers (as members of the club called themselves) feted Pulitzer Prize–winning author Marjorie Kinnan Rawlings, in 1939 for her book *The Yearling*. Rawlings had written to the Junipers noting that her concern

for authenticity was so strong that she was very pleased the Kentucky outdoorsmen at the camp enjoyed the book so much.

When Metro-Goldwyn-Mayer planned to make a movie of *The Yearling* in 1941, the movie company negotiated with the Juniper Club to film some of the movie on the grounds there and to build a 100-bed bunk house and accommodations for Spencer Tracy, who was to play Pa Baxter. When the project was postponed for various reasons, including the lack of deer in the area, Gregory Peck replaced Spencer Tracy in the role of Pa Baxter. Jane Wyman played the role of Ma Baxter, and child actor Claude Jarman Jr. played Jody. During the filming of *The Yearling* at the site, a barge sank in Silver Glen. It can still be seen today in the shallow water.

Today, the all-male club owns three thousand acres of land in the area, bounded by the Juniper River, Lake George, Silver Glen on the north, and Highway 19 on the west. Roads and sand trails criss-cross the land, which has many hunting stands, as well as eagles' nests, deer, and wild turkey.

The park at Silver Glen Springs, which is not very far from Lake George, has a Spring Boils Trail through the woods to the west of the headquarters that takes visitors along a boardwalk to the site of several sand boils, bubbling water that is rising to the surface through the sand. To the east of the springhead is an old Native American mound, although no sign indicates that since looters might be tempted to dig into the mound. In fact, Native American groups sometimes have special ceremonies there, with the permission of the park rangers. The park has day use only, no overnight camping.

Two miles north of there off Lake George is the entrance to Salt Springs. Again the entrance is difficult to see from the lake, and this particular one is quite shallow at normal river levels. I'm surprised that officials don't have this entrance deepened since boats with a draft of over three feet would have a very difficult time navigating the entrance. This three-mile-long run to the springhead recalls the image of Alph in Samuel Taylor Coleridge's "Kubla Khan":

> In Xanadu did Kubla Khan
> A stately pleasure-dome decree:
> Where Alph, the sacred river, ran
> Through caverns measureless of man
> Down to a sunless sea . . .
> A mighty fountain momently was forced:
> Amid whose swift half-intermitted burst
> Huge fragments vaulted like rebounding hail,
> Or chaffy grain beneath the thresher's flail.

Here are the words that Bartram wrote to describe Salt Springs: "About twenty yards from the upper edge of the bason, and directly opposite to the mouth or outlet to the creek, is a continual and amazing ebullition, where the waters are thrown up in such abundance and amazing force, as to jet and swell up two or three feet above the common surface: white sand and small particles of shells are thrown up with the waters, near to the top, when they diverge from the center, subside with the expanding flood, and gently sink again, forming a large rim or funnel round about the aperture or mouth of the fountain, which is a vast perforation through a bed of rocks, the ragged points of which are projected out on every side." Coleridge wrote his poem in 1797, five years after the publication of Bartram's *Travels*. In a well-written book about Bartram, *An Outdoor Guide to Bartram's Travels,* Charles Spornick and others note that Coleridge, although far away in England, used Bartram's image of the powerful spring as a figure for the imagination.

Near the entrance to Salt Springs run is a Timucuan mound on the northern shore. There are, in fact, three mounds. Visitors should not disturb the mounds or try to excavate them.

Salt Springs is unusual in that limestone rocks near the outpouring of the spring are close to the surface, and swimmers should take care when walking on the slippery rocks. Visitors should also look out for wildlife, especially the unfriendly kind, such as alligators. When we were there in 2003, we saw one alligator and two river otters, cute, shy creatures that eat fish and crayfish and an occasional mollusk. The spring is in Salt Springs Recreation Area in the Ocala National Forest, which President Theodore Roosevelt established in 1908. This first-magnitude spring pours out sixty-four million gallons of water a day.

The name of the spring and its salinity may go back to the fact that the water must pass through an old seashore, making it salty enough to support the crabs often seen in and around the springs. Most of the salinity in areas from Lake George north is derived from salt water springs that discharge into the river, and not from marine salinity currents.

Boaters near the different springs may notice boats from the Florida Fish and Wildlife Conservation Commission as they do their best to enforce laws about such things as safety equipment on boats and the speed of boats in manatee zones. The commission also stocks Lake George and other parts of the St. Johns River with different types of fish such

Salt Springs has a swimming area, but the very slippery rocks under the surface can cause problems.

as striped bass, which are bred in hatcheries and released as fingerlings. The fish tend to migrate to the cooler springs and tributaries during the heat of the summer, at which time the St. Johns becomes much warmer than the springs. In the winter, when the river cools down, the striped bass return to make Lake George a particularly good place for fishing. The extensive vegetation on the lake bottom provides good habitat for the fish, especially bass. Using shiners during the spring spawning season is particularly effective to catch trophy bass.

When we left Salt Springs and dashed across the northern rim of the lake in front of a very threatening storm cloud, we came upon Drayton Island. The island, named during the British occupation of Florida for a Chief Justice William Drayton, is three and a half miles long and consists of 1,870 acres. The Timucuans probably lived on Drayton Island, as evidenced by the pottery and shell tools they left behind.

The French in 1565 visited a Native American village on Drayton Island called Edelano, which they described as "the most delightful island in the world." When the British controlled Florida (1763–1783), Zephaniah Kingsley claimed the island, cleared the land, planted trees, and built a home along with some slave quarters. The southern tip of the island, Kinsley (or Kingsley) Point, honors him. In the 1880s, eight families from New England, consisting of around fifty people, were living in Edelano. It had its own post office and a population of 150 in 1889. The population seems to be much less than that today. A road runs the length of the island and passes an old abandoned airport with a grassy runway. Short dirt roads head off this road, each one leading to a house near the water. Because most of the island is privately owned, visitors should not wander off the road. At the northern end of Drayton Island we saw a tall, two-story house that was moved from the mainland in 2003—the house itself cost only $1 because its owner no longer wanted it on the mainland, but the move cost over $50,000. A ferry runs to and from the island from Georgetown during the day, but the schedule is subject to change. This is one of three vehicular ferries left in Florida, all of them on the St. Johns.

Boaters heading for the channel from Salt Springs and traversing south of Drayton should be wary of the pilings that extend quite far from the land. They are the remnants of a dock where steamers would moor as they took oranges from the island. One can still see oranges growing on the island, but the island is too far north these days for a profitable citrus industry since freezes regularly affect the area.

Just northwest of Drayton Island is Hog Island, no doubt named because of the wild hogs that used to roam there. The channel goes to the east of Drayton Island, and, although the river there is quite narrow, boaters should go that way, especially if their boats have a deep draft.

Putnam County claims to be the Bass Capital of the World, with some of the towns along the river also making that claim. Many fish camps line the east side of the river around Georgetown. We noticed that many of the restaurants and fish camps/motels along this stretch of the water advertised their address in terms of a street number for those approaching by car and a marker number for those approaching by boat. Many places along the way allowed/encouraged boaters to tie up, as we often did, and have a meal or spend the night.

The west side of the river and Hog Island are undeveloped and have been the place where visitors have seen wild hogs, deer, even maybe a panther. Panthers have long since gone and are pretty much found only in southwest Florida. Wild hogs, which have been hunted for decades throughout the state, may have made their way to the isolated island in search of food. Deer are plentiful throughout Florida, including this island, which is far enough from the mainland and the main channel of the St. Johns as to provide the creatures some protection.

Georgetown, the first town we encountered heading north from Lake George, took its name from King George III during the British occupation of Florida in the eighteenth century. The town used to have a box-making factory, a packing house, and a port for boats going between Jacksonville and Sanford, but today it is mostly a fishing village with small homes and citrus groves. A small marina at Georgetown is where my two boating companions and I took refuge from a heavy but short-lived summer storm as we headed north. The settlement of Lake George two miles south of Georgetown is a growing community established in 1872.

Another small settlement just to the north of Georgetown along the river is Fruitland, which traces its history to 1856, when it was first settled. The name testifies to the many orange groves which used to be there but which were devastated by some very bad freezes in the early twentieth century. Nearby used to lie Sulphur Springs, where religious camp meetings attracted as many as four hundred people.

On the western shore above Georgetown and southwest of Fruitland is Fort Gates, a supply post established in 1835 during the Second Seminole War, although the definitive history of Putnam County, *The River Flows North*, indicates the British may have established a fort there in the 1780s

The elegant house is a gothic–type house.

and named it after Sir Thomas Gates, onetime governor of Virginia. Today, a ferry runs between Fort Gates and the other side of the river west of Mount Royal. It is the second of three vehicular ferries left in Florida and saves drivers much time since the nearest bridges are thirty miles in either direction.

Settlers began moving into Fort Gates before the Civil War. The Confederates had a hospital there, and by the 1880s forty families were living at the site. Today, a small group of elegant, Victorian-style houses line the shore. The most prominent house, called the Palmettos, was built in 1878 and may be the fanciest gothic mansion on the whole river. The three-story building next door housed a bowling alley, billiard room, and six guest rooms on the upper floor.

To the northwest of Fruitland, just as the river turns sharply to the west, on the eastern shore of the river near flashing green marker 63 is Mount Royal, one of the most impressive Native American middens along the river. The Mount Royal site, which is on the National Register of Historic Places, is several hundred yards off the river on the eastern bank. John and William Bartram described it in 1766 as an "Indian tumulus, which was about 100 yards in diameter, nearly round, and near twenty feet high."

Archaeologists have found remains of a Spanish mission there, one of the many sites along the river where missionaries proselytized among the Native Americans. Today, the State of Florida owns the mound, which is a little over one acre in size, although the surrounding causeway and middens are privately owned. Native Americans occupied the site four thousand years ago. They fished, gathered shellfish, hunted, and collected plants. A large number of Native Americans lived in the vicinity around A.D. 500.

The presence of copper at the site indicates that the mound was a major center of Native American life in the area because copper was rare and valuable to those people. The site of the mound was strategic in that the people living there could control traffic to and from central Florida along the river.

The chiefs there had the mound built to indicate their importance and that of both their ancestors and descendants. The tribe placed the mortal remains of the chief and the chief's family members, along with artifacts, in the mound, which became larger with more and more burials. The members of the tribe considered the mound as a holy site. Archaeologists indicate that the heyday of the mound was around A.D. 1050 and 1300.

The first Europeans in this area, French explorers coming from Fort Caroline near the mouth of the St. Johns, arrived at the site in 1565, at which time it was a Timucuan village named Enacape. The French went to Enacape a second time under René de Laudonnière to gather corn for the French colonists at Fort Caroline, who were starving because they did not plant enough crops and could not obtain food from the Native Americans, with whom they were at odds.

Spanish missionaries established the mission of San Antonio de Enacape at Mount Royal. The Franciscans began this mission, sometimes called Anacabila, in 1595. Around 1656, the Native Americans living at the mission were moved by the Spanish north along the St. Johns to the mission of San Diego de Salamototo, where they operated a ferry across the river near present-day Orangedale, east of Green Cove Springs. In the 1680s, Yamasees from the Georgia coast were at Mount Royal. By the early 1700s, the mission there was abandoned.

The Northeast Florida Anthropological Society restored the Mount Royal mound in the early 1970s, and it was added to the National Register of Historic Places in 1973. Development on the surrounding valuable land continues, but a fence around the mound helps protect it to some extent.

When the river turns due north again, opens up into Little Lake George, and widens to over a mile across, the land due west is Norwalk, named by settlers from Norwalk, Connecticut, in the late nineteenth century.

Most of them moved out when severe freezes hit the area, but today the town is slowly recovering.

Just as the river turns north and just north of Norwalk Point is Croaker Hole, an artesian spring that pumps over fifty million gallons of fresh water into the St. Johns every day. The many fish there (thus its name) often attract fishermen in their boats. Divers can go down over seventy feet to the cave until the power of the outrushing water forces them to the surface. While the water near the surface is typically murky, the water near the river bottom is crystal clear.

by land from Lake George to Fruitland

From Astor on the west side of the river, drivers can go up along Lake George and visit three very beautiful springs. First go west on SR 40 for about eight miles, then north on SR 19.

Juniper Springs is off SR 40 about 4.5 miles west of SR 19. The park is very popular much of the year and has a spring-fed pool for swimming.

To reach Silver Glen Springs Park, go back to SR 19, north about 5.8 miles (past Juniper Wayside Park), and into the state park on the right. Across SR 19 from the entrance to Silver Glen Springs Park is a sign for the Yearling Trail in the Ocala National Forest. The hiking trail extends for about six miles into the forest. One of its highlights is Pat's Island, a place associated with author Marjorie Kinnan Rawlings and the Reuben Long family that she wrote about in *The Yearling*. About ten miles further up SR 19 is the entrance on the right to Salt Springs.

Across from the park and a little to the north on the left is a shopping center that has a visitor center for the Ocala National Forest. About ten miles north of there on SR 19 is the entrance on the left to Rodman Dam and on the right to Rodeheaver Boys Ranch. A paved road to the west before the bridge leads to the Senator George Kirkpatrick Dam/Rodman Spillway, a favorite place for fishermen and boaters. The Rodman Campground has thirty-nine campsites, a hiking trail, picnic shelters, and restrooms.

On the east side of Lake George is mostly swampy land, but U.S. 17 parallels the lake. At Seville SR 305 heads west to the lake, ending at Pine Island Resort, a collection of trailers and small homes and a boat ramp that provides access to the lake. Smaller, paved roads lead north to the small communities of Lake George Point and Georgetown. SR 309 leads up to Fruitland.

Those traveling by car can more easily visit Mount Royal than those traveling by boat since the mound is inland and homes close to the water can block the view of boaters. The mound itself is fenced in to keep out looters, but you can easily drive around it. This is one of my favorite mounds in all of Florida because of its strategic position at the northern tip of Lake George, its well-preserved and off-limits status, and its interesting history.

5 Little Lake George to East Palatka

"Presently we rounded the raft [of pine logs], abandoned the broad and garish highway of the St. Johns, and turned off to the right into the narrow lane of the Ocklawaha, the sweetest water-lane in the world, . . . as if a typical woods-stroll had taken shape and as if God had turned into water and trees the recollection of some meditative ramble through the lonely seclusions of His own soul."

—*Sidney Lanier,* Florida: Its Scenery, Climate, and History

by water from Little Lake George to East Palatka

The section of the St. Johns River from Lake George to East Palatka, while praised effusively by poet Sidney Lanier, was the subject of a controversial proposal for a man-made project which would have changed the St. Johns irreparably. It also witnessed one of the most remarkable river battles in the Civil War.

The river changes directions drastically as you go up to Palatka. At first, the channel goes due north from Little Lake George to the entrance to the Ocklawaha River. Then it zigzags a little to Buffalo Point, where it takes a major east turn. The name of the water at the southeastern part of Little Lake George, Buzzard Roost Cove, no doubt goes back to an early explorer who noticed buzzards in the area, which is very swampy and uninhabited.

Beecher Point opposite the Ocklawaha River and also Beecher Spring south of Welaka were named in honor of famed preacher Henry Ward Beecher and his sister, author Harriet Beecher Stowe, who visited the area together.

At marker 52 is the entrance on the western side of the river to the Ocklawaha River, one of the most important rivers in the history of Florida tourism. Boaters can easily miss the entrance since it is off to the west of the channel and has only a small marker near the land, but we could not see any sign or marker in the river itself to indicate the entrance. Hyacinth pads marked the entrance, and because the hyacinth was so thick, we could see why many boaters avoided this river. Paddle wheel steamboats used to go up this river in the nineteenth century, taking scores of tourists, many of whom had boarded in Jacksonville. Before the building of dams, they could have gone all the way to Silver Springs. Marjorie Kinnan Rawlings turned up this river from the St. Johns on her memorable trip in 1933. The trip renewed her spirit and made her appreciate Cross Creek and all it offered: "Because I had known intimately a river, the earth pulsed under me," she wrote in her nonfiction *Cross Creek*.

The St. Johns has had many uses. Cypress loggers used it to float felled trees to markets down the river. Passengers on the steamers going into the interior would sometimes stand on the top of the boats and shoot gators and fish and birds along the way, just for the fun of it. Famed poet Sidney Lanier (1842–1881), whose remarks are at the beginning of this chapter, made the trip and wrote about it in a Florida guidebook that a

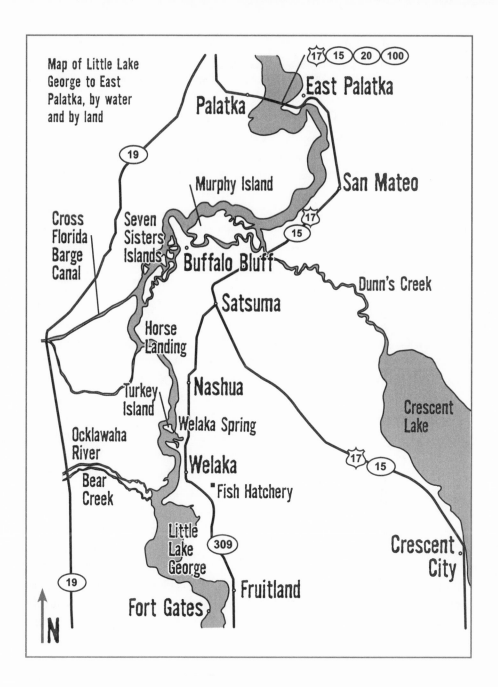

Map of Little Lake George to East Palatka, by water and by land

railroad company commissioned. Today, the Ocklawaha is almost totally deserted. In fact, we did not see a single boat on the river that day.

The Ocklawaha, this tributary of the St. Johns, is really amazing. Some twenty artesian springs feed into it, including the powerful one at Silver

Springs, which alone pours 540 million gallons of fresh water every day. The river is one of the most important and strongest feeders of the St. Johns. Its name used to be spelled "Oklawaha" for many years until the U.S. Board of Geographic Names restored the "c" in 1992 at the request of historians and local officials. The name derives from the Creek *aklowahe*, which means "muddy." A town in Marion County and the lake formed by the Rodman Reservoir also have the same name.

If you make the long water trip up the Ocklawaha to Silver Springs State Park—which exists since the nineteenth century—you will be rewarded with glass-bottom boats, alligator shows, and music concerts.

The Rodman Dam is at the entrance to Lake Ocklawaha from the Ocklawaha River, and boaters can travel the five miles between the dam and SR 19 on a clearly marked channel. The mouth of the Ocklawaha was totally deserted when we passed it, but according to Charles Bennett's *Twelve on the River St. Johns,* a powerful chief, Olata Ouae Outina, once had his principal village near the site. From there he and his followers fought battles with other tribes, including Saturiba, the head of the Timucuans who befriended the French when they arrived at the mouth of the St. Johns in the early 1560s.

Doug Stamm, in his *Springs of Florida,* mentions how American shad have been known to enter the St. Johns from the Atlantic Ocean, swim a hundred miles up to the Ocklawaha, continue through to the Silver River and Silver Springs, spawn, and then return down the St. Johns.

To the northeast is one of the larger towns in the area: Welaka, whose original name was Mount Tucker, after a Lord Tucker who occupied the land there during the British occupation of Florida. The name Welaka comes from a combination of Native-American words meaning "tide or intermittent springs." *Welaka* or *Ylacco* is what the Seminoles called the St. Johns River. The term may also mean "river of lakes," which is appropriate. It is in fact the name of Bill Belleville's excellent book about the St. Johns. The present name of the St. Johns River comes from the Spanish mission *San Juan del Puerto* (St. John of the Harbor), which Franciscan missionaries established on San Juan Island at the mouth of the river in 1595. The mission name, in fact, superseded the French name of the river, *Rivière de Mai* (River of May), for when they arrived there, May 1, 1562 and the earlier Spanish name of *San Mateo.*

During the Civil War, federal troops occupied an outpost near Welaka in an attempt to stop the flow of food and supplies meant for the Confederates on the river. After the war, families moved into the area and made a living from growing citrus (until freezes drove them out) and fishing, which has continued to provide a good living to those with fish camps and facilities along the river. The many fish camps and motels in the area continue to attest to that, especially as the town advertises itself as "the Bass Capital of the World." Remnants of the O.H. Morris Crab Company and the Welaka Seafood Company point to a time when workers processed crab, Florida shad, and herring roe for shipping to stores and restaurants around the country. Welaka Springs is north of the town, but—like all the springs north of Lake George, with the exception of Green Cove Springs—they provide relatively little water to the St. Johns.

Near marker 58 at the southwestern edge of Little Lake George south of Welaka is Croaker Hole, a freshwater spring that is difficult to find. Local divers can dive 45 feet or more into the spring. The hole is a popular place for striped bass and sunshine bass, which like to congregate in creeks with cool-water discharges and in large springs, such as Croaker Hole, during the summer. We learned from a local guide that one way fishermen try to outwit/lure mullet is to come to the river one day and put a feed bag in the water. The next day they return and collect the fish caught in the bag.

Between Welaka and Welaka Springs is Stephens Point, a promontory forcing the river to veer to the west for a short distance. Stephens Point was named after a local family that can be traced back to the Civil War.

Turkey Island in the middle of the river forces boaters to go one way or the other, most likely to the western side instead of the longer path to the east, toward Welaka Springs. The land on the western side from below the Ocklawaha to north of the barge canal is mostly swamp, although Rodeheaver Boys Ranch is situated there.

Three miles north of Welaka is Horse Landing on the west side of the St. Johns between markers 37 and 35. There in May 1864, Confederate cavalry under the command of the brilliant Captain J.J. Dickison sank a Union side-wheel tug, the *Columbine,* in what some historians call "the major Confederate naval victory in Florida." The 117-foot-long wooden vessel, which drew six feet of water, was to be used by Union troops to tow coal vessels, patrol the St. Johns, attack Confederate ships in the river, and transport goods and troops.

Enemy sharpshooters lying in wait along the river disabled the *Columbine* when it came within sixty yards of shore, and forced its crew to flee. The Confederates stripped the vessel of everything useful and then burned the wooden boat to keep it from being raised by the Union troops. Captain Dickison had his men take the *Columbine*'s lifeboat and sink it in a lake near Palatka. The destruction of the *Columbine* did not have much effect on the outcome of the war, but it did rally Floridians behind Captain Dickison and gave his troops a much-needed morale booster in the waning months of the war. The relic of the *Columbine* rested for over one hundred years in the St. Johns until divers chanced upon her in the 1970s, but very little is left of the vessel.

Each fall, usually in November, over a thousand participants re-enact the Battle of Horse Landing. The re-enactment, which takes place at Rodeheaver Boys Ranch, also features displays of military camp life, cannon firing, cavalry charges, infantry tactics, and civilian life during the Civil War.

To the west of marker 33 is the beginning of the famous (or infamous) Cross Florida Barge Canal, one of the most controversial projects in the history of this state. For the past hundred years, engineers looking at Central Florida, with its many lakes and rivers, envisioned a canal that would bisect the state, connect the Atlantic Ocean with the Gulf of Mexico, lessen the time needed for ships to go around the state, and thus save lots of money and time.

During World War II, when U-boats threatened ships along the eastern coast, the U.S. Congress, by a one-vote margin, finally authorized the building of such a canal. In 1964, the U.S. Army Corps of Engineers began construction of the Cross Florida Barge Canal. In 1968, engineers finished the Rodman Dam and Reservoir, destroying nine thousand acres of productive river and floodplain forest along sixteen miles of the Ocklawaha River.

The proposed Cross Florida Barge Canal was probably the single most dangerous threat to the water resources of the state in the twentieth century. When concerned individuals realized how the canal would threaten the diverse, productive river forest along the Ocklawaha River, they formed the Florida Defenders of the Environment to protect the swamp. Scientists studied the importance of swamps to the environment and concluded that they are necessary for the purification of water and the maintenance of wildlife, but their studies came too late to save the swamp along the proposed canal as engineers formed Lake Ocklawaha.

Those studies did lead to the saving of other swamps, such as Big Cypress Swamp in southwest Florida in the 1970s and Green Swamp in central Florida, which were named areas of critical state concern.

Big Cypress became a national preserve as private, state, and federal interests cooperated to save the swamp. Still, environmentalists worried whether it was too late to stop the Barge Canal.

At first, a legal challenge by the Environmental Defense Fund and Florida Defenders of the Environment stopped construction of the Cross Florida Barge Canal in 1971, but it took another nineteen years, a $2.5 million restudy by the U.S. Corps of Engineers, and public opposition to the Barge Canal to finally ban it in 1990. Environmentalists could finally begin to restore the damaged Ocklawaha.

State and federal bills transformed the former canal lands into the Cross State Greenbelt for Conservation and Recreation (later named the Marjorie Harris Carr Cross Florida Greenway for the person who led the fight to stop the canal project), a 110-mile-long, 75,000-acre greenway that goes from the Gulf of Mexico to the St. Johns River. This was Florida's first official greenway and remains the centerpiece of the state's open space dedicated to conservation and recreation.

About a mile and a half up the remnants of the canal from the St. Johns is the Henry Holland Buckman Lock, which allows boats to go to and from Lake Ocklawaha farther west. This lake was created when Rodman Dam and Eureka Dam bottled up fourteen square miles of the floodplain. The lock was closed for repairs when we were there, but a guide at the visitors center thought it would eventually open. The good fishing in the lake and around the Rodman Reservoir has created sharp differences of opinion between those who want to restore the Ocklawaha River and those who want to keep the dams intact.

Stokes Island just north of the Barge Canal is the traditional site of Spaulding's Lower Trading Store, which William Bartram visited in 1774. It was from there that he prepared and shipped to London many of the plants he had collected and which his royal sponsors eagerly awaited. Bartram used the Lower Trading Store as the headquarters from which he traveled west to Alachua.

North of here, the river begins a dramatic turn to the east before resuming its northerly run near San Mateo. The river passes between Stokes Island on the left (west) and Trout Island/Seven Sisters Islands on the right. My companions and I headed back among the Seven Sisters to an isolated community at Barrentine Creek, a collection of houses facing the river, many of which had boats. All down the river we found picturesque settlements, places with ideal locations for fishing and boating but out of the way and not yet discovered by tourists.

An eighty-acre estate on the river in this vicinity used to be called "Hermit's Cove" by Tyler Gatewood Kent (1911–1988), an American charged with spying for the Nazis during World War II while he served at the American embassy in London. He lived there while working as the publisher from 1959 to 1962 of the *Putnam County Weekly Sun,* a newspaper famous for its extremist political views.

The railroad passes just north of there to Buffalo Bluff, where it crosses the St. Johns by a bascule bridge. The turn around Buffalo Bluff is so sharp that long barges such as those carrying fuel to Sanford have to be very careful. One wonders why engineers did not cut through the peninsula of Buffalo Bluff, as they did north of Volusia/Astor, to avoid making the sharp turns around Morrison Island.

Boaters who have the time can go around the very large Murphy Island and the smaller Polly Island and Rat Island. We did that, heading along the southern shore of Murphy Island until we reached Dunn's Creek. Murphy Island, which has a large Native American mound in the middle, may have been where the white proprietors of Spalding's Lower Store hid their goods in the 1770s when they feared an attack by the Native Americans.

We came out on Dunn's Creek just about where the bridge for highways 15/17 crosses over. While the land to the north of the creek has houses and canals, the land to the south is swampy. In 1999, the Nature Conservancy bought over six thousand acres along the creek as part of the state's Dunn's Creek Conservation and Recreation Land Project. Seven miles of that land borders the creek. Then, in 2001, the Nature Conservancy sold the land to the state for preservation. Funds from the sale will go into an endowment that will enable the Conservancy to continue providing restoration and management services at no cost to the public. The area that will be protected forever has nineteen native habitats, including forested wetlands, longleaf pine, and wiregrass sandhills. The area also provides habitat for gopher tortoises, wading and migratory birds, and West Indian manatees. Gopher tortoises live in burrows, which they dig out of the dirt with their strong, front feet, and share their underground homes with snakes, mammals, frogs, and many different invertebrates.

We stopped at a fish camp to get fuel and supplies before heading to Crescent Lake. We learned that the Florida Fish and Wildlife Conservation Commission named Dunn's Creek one of the best places in Florida to catch bullhead, channel, and white catfish, and that fishermen can catch small catfish all year long but the best time is in spring and fall. The creek meanders back to Crescent Lake.

During the Civil War, Dunn's Creek was the site of the deliberate scuttling of one of the most famous yachts in the world, the *America,* as Confederate sailors tried to keep the boat out of the hands of Union troops who were about to enter Jacksonville. The history of the boat is the subject of books and articles. In 1851, boat builders in New York had built a schooner yacht known for a long bow and her ability to carry a tall rig. After her launch, the *America* sailed for England, the first vessel ever to cross an ocean for interna-

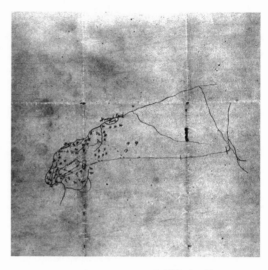

A 1860s handdrawn map of Dunn's Creek by George Washington Scott.

tional competition. There, she entered an open regatta and easily won, receiving an ornate prize called the Royal Yacht Squadron 100 Guineas Cup, so named for what it cost to have it made. The trophy would be renamed The America's Cup and would remain in American hands until the Australians won it in 1983, only to lose it back to the United States four years later.

After several owners bought the boat, it wound up in the American Civil War on the side of the Confederacy as the *Memphis.* She was stationed in Jacksonville in 1862, unable to escape into the Atlantic because of the tightening of the Union blockade. As Union troops were about to enter Jacksonville, Confederate sailors took the *Memphis* up the St. Johns and into Dunn's Creek, where they sank her. A Union search party found the sunken boat, carefully raised her, took her back to Jacksonville, renamed her *America,* and put her into service as part of the Union blockade. After the war, she became a private yacht, but ended up at the U.S. Naval Academy in Annapolis, Maryland, where a snowstorm collapsed her protecting shed in 1942 and destroyed the yacht beyond repair.

We headed into Crescent Lake for what we thought would be a leisurely tour of the lake and lunch at Crescent City. But we didn't check the weather report, which we definitely should have done.

Crescent Lake is about sixteen thousand acres in size, making it one of the largest in Florida. Its name, which used to be Dunn's Lake, was changed by a resident from New York City for its crescent moon shape, which also gave its name to the largest town, which lies at the southwestern end of the lake. Although a few white settlers had lived in the area before the Civil War, afterwards many people moved in to raise vegetables and cattle and take advantage of the lake, with its connection to Jacksonville.

Among the houses near the lake worth mentioning is the Hubbard House at 600 North Park Street, the home of a famous American entomologist, Henry Guernsey Hubbard (1850–1899). Among the most famous residents was A. Philip Randolph (1889–1979), who organized the Brotherhood of Sleeping Car Porters, the first major black labor union; in 1963, he was the chairman of the March on Washington for Jobs and Freedom, and introduced Dr. Martin Luther King Jr. to make his "I Have a Dream" speech.

Another prominent resident was photographer F.B. Pines, who operated the only floating photograph gallery on the St. Johns River in the 1870s. In 1884, after only six years of taking photographs on the river, he had done so well that he wanted to retire, and therefore put out the following ad:

> For Sale. The only floating photograph gallery on the St. Johns River. A No. 1 reputation; first-class instruments; operating room, 35 feet long; good dark room, dining room and kitchen; sleeping accommodations for two besides one elegant stateroom, light 10 x 12, just the thing for those in search of health and a good business. Price complete, $1,200; without instruments, $800. Reasons for selling, owner wishes to retire.

Unfortunately for Mr. Pines, no one came up with the right price, and he had to continue working until 1898, when he was finally able to dispose of his equipment.

The building which now houses the Three Bananas Restaurant used to be a warehouse where bare-knuckle fights were held in the 1940s. One remnant of the warehouse is a series of pilings in the lake nearby. There was a railroad at the warehouse from which local planters shipped out citrus by train up to Jacksonville.

In the middle of Crescent Lake is Bear Island, which is half in Putnam County and half in Flagler County and has a runway that World War II fighter pilots used in their training because it resembled an aircraft

carrier in size. There are also two shacks and a Native American mound on the island.

The east side of Crescent Lake, which is part of Flagler County, is mostly swampy and uninhabited. The west side leads to Pomono Park, a town settled by former Union soldiers and their families from New England after the Civil War. That town is closer to Lake Broward than to Crescent Lake.

Crescent Lake can be treacherous during storms, as my boating companions and I discovered when a sudden summer storm caught us in the middle and drenched us as we raced back to Dunn's Creek. We resolved to be more aware of the weather reports for the rest of our trip.

Back in the St. Johns River, the large Murphy Island is uninhabited, owned by the government. Two miles east of there along the St. Johns is the small settlement of Edgewater, the place where Mrs. Fuller put her hyacinths into the river after obtaining samples of the pretty flower from the 1884 World's Exposition in New Orleans (for more details about the pernicious hyacinth, see chapter one).

As the river turns north once again, the town of San Mateo begins on the east bank. Near this site along the river was Rollestown or Rollston, one of the most remarkable attempts during the British occupation to grow crops in Florida. Denys Rolle, an English philanthropist and member of parliament, established a plantation there in 1765 and named it Charlotta;

Small creeks off the main river often led to fish camps.

he later changed the name to Charlotia. Rolle, whom Cabell and Hanna describe in *The St. Johns : A Parade of Diversities* (1943) as a "high-nosed and pale-eyed altruist, who was bent upon making his fellow creatures more virtuous and more happy, whether they liked it or not," populated his town with forty prosti-tutes, pickpockets, and beggars from the slums of London. He also brought slaves, especially after the Londoners protested about the hard work of clearing the swamps and fled to St. Augustine. Eventually buying some eighty thousand acres in the area, Rolle succeeded in producing rice, corn, beef, lumber, and naval stores, but gave up and left for the Bahamas with his slaves when Spain reacquired Florida in 1783.

While the western bank is mostly swampy and uninhabited, the east side up toward East Palatka has more and more homes and motels and restaurants. Just north of Rivercrest, the river turns sharply to the west around a pointy peninsula, heads due west for a mile, then heads north to Palatka.

At East Palatka, the river actually turns due south at the ominous-sounding Devil's Elbow, a very sharp peninsula jutting up toward East Palatka on the southern bank of the river. The turn is so abrupt, in fact, that one wonders if engineers ever considered cutting through the narrow peninsula jutting up from the western bank in order to make the trip less dangerous for the large barges heading in either direction.

East Palatka, while not inside the city limits of Palatka, has begun to establish an identity of its own, with more and more restaurants and

homes being built there. Near the Devil's Elbow is where the father of Palatka native General Joseph W. "Vinegar Joe" Stilwell owned eight acres. General Joseph Stilwell was the American commander in the China-Burma-India theater during World War II.

The view from River Street is quite good.

The cove due south of Palatka and before the river, which goes under the bridge, is Wilson Cove, possibly named after one of Palatka's most important businesses, the Wilson Cypress Company. Founded in 1889, the company was at one time the second-largest business of its kind in the world. Marjorie Kinnan Rawlings mentioned the company in her first published novel, *South Moon Under.*

River navigation charts indicate that many sunken steamboats are scattered around Wilson Cove, a reminder of the days when such vessels plied the waters between Jacksonville and Palatka and further south. On the shore behind the cove is one of Palatka's prettiest streets—River Street, which still has large Victorian houses that hearken back to the days when Palatka was known as "Gem City of the St. Johns."

by land from Little Lake George to East Palatka

The eastern bank of the river has towns all along SR 309. North of Fruitland, which is north of Georgetown, visitors can tour the Welaka National Fish Hatchery and see how millions of fish are reared in the two sections behind the office building. The hatchery's purpose expanded from restocking Florida's streams and lakes to conserving them. Nearby Beecher Spring supplies nine million gallons of fresh water a day to the facility. Beecher Spring has an observation tower for nature watching.

The first major town north of Fruitland is Welaka, which has fish camps and motels and small restaurants that specialize in fresh fish from the river. North of that is Nashua, which was settled by northerners who grew oranges in the second half of the nineteenth century. Planters also planted tung oil trees. Another town with a northern name is Saratoga on the St. Johns to the northwest of Nashua.

North of Nashua, SR 309 connects with Highways 15/17, which leads into Satsuma about two miles from the river. The town takes its name from the special type of orange/tangerine grown there. Beginning in 1914, camphor berries were raised there until competition from abroad and synthetic camphor put the camphor plantation out of business. The railroad passes through Satsuma toward Buffalo Bluff on the St. Johns and then over the river to Palatka.

Highway 15/17 parallels the St. Johns River from Satsuma to Palatka. In East Palatka at a wayside park on the west side of the highway are two historic markers: one for William Bartram and the other for Rollestown, which Denys Rolle founded with high hopes. Today, a large electrical facility built by Florida Power and Light occupies the site of Rollestown. Mrs. Henry Ward Beecher (1812–1897), the wife of one of the century's most famous preachers, stayed at Rollestown in a cottage built from the remains of Rolle's house as she wrote *Letters from Florida* (1879).

Driving north from Salt Springs on US 19 on the west side of the St. Johns River, you will find mostly uninhabited land that is part of the Ocala National Forest. Between Salt Springs and the bridge over the Barge Canal is the Caravelle Wildlife Management Area, located between the Ocklawaha and St. Johns Rivers. The 25,000-acre site has hardwood river swamps, pine flatwoods, and improved pastures, and offers hiking, hunting, and nature observation, as well as supervised hunting parties.

Horses are welcome, and ample space is available for parking trailers. The site offers good fishing and bird-watching experiences, especially in the spring when swallow-tailed kites circle the pastures. These beautiful birds with their black-and-white plumage, tapering wings, and deeply forked tail stay airborne much of the time, feeding on dragonflies, lizards, snakes, frogs, and nestling birds, while occasionally skimming over water and scooping up water in their beak.

Further north on SR 19 and just before the bridge over the canal you can go west on Rodman Dam Road to reach the dam. In the spillway below the dam, fishermen try their luck. Boaters use the lake above the dam.

Off to the east of SR 19 before the canal is the road to Horse Landing, the site of the Rodeheaver Boys Ranch, which Homer Rodeheaver and Harry Westbury opened in 1950 for neglected and dependent boys aged seven to eighteen. President Lyndon Johnson visited the ranch in 1964 when he officially began the construction of the controversial Cross-Florida Barge Canal. The baseball field there, called Little Yankee Field, was built in 1978 with funds from George Steinbrenner, the owner of the New York Yankees. The ranch, whose motto is "It is Better to Build Boys Than to Mend Men," accepts no county, state, or federal funding, instead relying on private donations and fundraising activities.

The bridge over the canal a little further on SR 19 gives drivers good views of the straight canal on each side. About 2.4 miles further north on the right is the entrance to the Marjorie Harris Carr Visitor Center, which has good displays about the Cross Florida Greenway and an overlook near the Buckman Lock on the canal. The Greenway, which retains many parts of the former Cross-Florida Barge Canal while also joining rivers and parks along the way, goes from Putnam County across the state to Levy County and Citrus County. The eastern end of the Greenway begins at the St. Johns River and borders the Ocala National Forest following the Ocklawaha River floodplain. After the Barge Canal was stopped in 1990, the land was turned over to Florida for use as a conservation and recreation area. Today, the Florida Department of Environmental Protection's Office of Greenways and Trails manages the corridor. Palatka is about 8.4 miles north on SR 19.

6 Palatka to Green Cove Springs

"At Palatka, the St. Johns makes an elbow turn such as pushes its banks a full mile apart. Rafts of huge cypress logs towed down the river are here cut (it is instructive to reflect) into forty million feet of lumber annually, in what is reported to be the largest cypress mill in the world. (Nothing in Florida, let it be explained, is ever described, by the peace-loving, without a suitable coalescence of superlatives.)"

—*Cabell and Hanna,* The St. Johns

by water from Palatka to Green Cove Springs

Palatka has had several births and rebirths. Its name derives from a Seminole word, *pilotaikita,* meaning "ferry," "food," or "crossing." Early white settlers shortened the word to "Pilatka," but later changed it to its present spelling when postal authorities complained that it was too close to Picolata, farther down the river. Settlers established a trading post there in 1821, but Native Americans burned it down in 1836. Two years later, federal troops established Fort Shannon on the left bank of the St. Johns River to serve as a quartermaster depot during the Second Seminole War (1835–1842). Officers stationed at the fort included Zachary Taylor, Winfield Scott, and William Tecumseh Sherman. The fort was abandoned in 1843 and relative stability returned to the area, allowing settlers to move in.

The city's strategic location on the St. Johns, with its accessibility to Jacksonville via steamboat and its proximity to St. Augustine, made Palatka one of the most important tourist destinations along the river in the second half of the nineteenth century. When the railroad made the steamboat obsolete, timber companies moved in, cut down most of the surrounding trees, and built papermaking companies that belched noxious fumes into the air for decades. Only in the last few decades has Palatka gotten rid of most of the polluting companies and concentrated on its

A swing by the dock provides a beautiful view of the river.

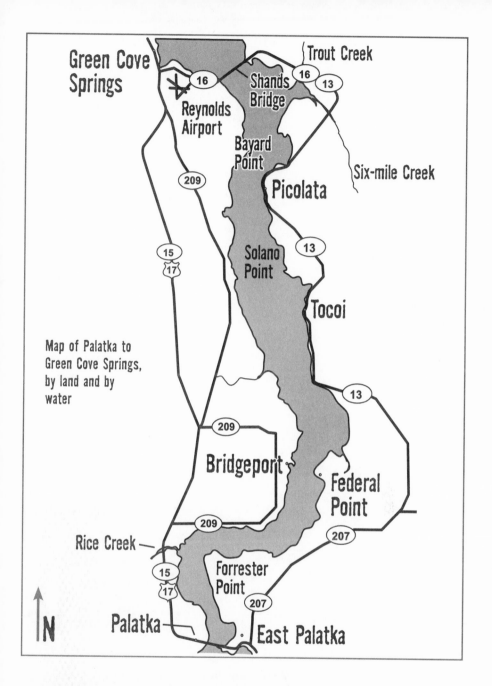

Map of Palatka to Green Cove Springs, by land and by water

strategic location on the St. Johns to attract visitors, students (to the St. Johns River Community College), and full-time residents.

Boaters today can use the municipal docks in Palatka, but the $25-a-night fee and the necessity to get a permit from city hall make it an unwelcome place. During the times I have been in the city, I have never seen any boaters using the docks overnight, perhaps discouraged by the high fee. It seemed to me such a departure from the years when Palatka welcomed the steamers coming down from Jacksonville with many tourists and visitors.

The St. Johns from Palatka to Mayport widens appreciably, sometimes spanning two miles. Some twelve streams empty into the St. Johns but do not provide as much water as the springs south of here, especially the first-magnitude springs like Blue Spring, Silver Glen Springs, and Silver Springs.

At marker 43, near the power plant, the river heads due east, then resumes its northerly run. Each promontory jutting into the river seems to have "Point" in its name: Forrester Point, Russels Point, Myrtlewood Point, Dancy Point, etc.—all related to area homeowners' names. One wonders about the origin of some names on the west bank, such as Ninemile Point and Deadman Point. The effect of ocean tides can be felt this far inland from the Atlantic; there is about a one-foot difference between low and high tides. Saltwater fish have also been found in the area as they make their way up the broad river relatively unimpeded.

Some of the houses on the west shore are old, but elegant.

We boated over to Rice Creek north of Palatka, but we had to be careful to mind the channel, even in our relatively shallow-draft

boat, because the navigation charts indicate some very shallow water on each side of the channel. We noticed the power plant and recalled the days of the paper mills, when the skies above this area were full of terrible-smelling fumes.

The fisherman takes his livelihood from the river.

I know that each little cove and point probably has an interesting story, but very few of the newer residents seem to know them. For example, I read in Brian Michaels' *The River Flows North,* that Dancy Point, just where the river begins to turn north again east of Grandview, was named after Francis Dancy, a West Point graduate who served as Surveyor General of Florida in the early nineteenth century and who gave the Confederates the official records he had during the Civil War. Because he was too old to serve in that war, he and his family settled down at Orange Mills just south of Dancy Point. That same area is where Zephaniah Kingsley planted the first commercial orange grove in Florida, but a freeze later wiped out the citrus trees and led to the building of a large sawmill there.

Across from Federal Point is Bridgeport on the west shore, a settlement that has had several names: Henderson's Point (for the owner), Magnolia Point (for the surrounding trees), Palmetto Bluff (also for the trees), Brookland (for a nearby stream), and finally Bridgeport (for the Connecticut city where the new owner came from). In the late nineteenth century, the place had an iron works, sawmills, a foundry, a machine shop, a railway, a moss factory, a furniture factory, and a brickyard. Today, homes make up the area.

Beyond Federal Point on the east side, we boated up Deep Creek, so called because it is eighteen to twenty feet deep. We saw from our nautical maps that it goes back into St. Johns County, especially the potato-growing land around Hastings and Spud. The presence of fishermen, even on a weekday, attests to the abundant fish in the creek.

At Tocoi we saw pilings in the water, perhaps a remnant of the ferry dock where passengers would disembark for the overland trip to St. Augustine. My guide to the onomastics of the state, Allen Morris's *Florida Place Names*, tells me that "Tocoi" comes from a Native American name for "water lily." I learn from the WPA guidebook, *Florida: A Guide to the Southernmost State* (1949), that a Native American village used to be here, as well as a Franciscan mission during the Spanish occupation. The mission, called San Diego de Salamototo, was one of many that stretched west from St. Augustine to the Apalachicola River. Michael Gannon pointed out in *The Cross in the Sand* and *Florida: A Short History* that the Franciscans, who first arrived in 1573, succeeded in imparting the Christian faith to twenty-six thousand Native Americans and in teaching them methods of European farming, cattle raising, carpentry, weaving, reading, and writing.

After the Civil War, a combination of mule power and railroad took passengers between Tocoi and St. Augustine, fifteen miles away on the Atlantic coast. That road caused Picolata, which is further down the river, to decline in importance. When Henry Flagler completed his railroad from Jacksonville to St. Augustine around 1888, Tocoi itself declined as passengers chose the speed of the railroad over the steamboat.

Tocoi was the place where the grandfather of author John Steinbeck settled in the 1850s with the intention of retiring after many dangerous adventures in the Holy Land. When the Civil War broke out, Confederate soldiers impressed the grandfather, also named John Steinbeck, into the war. Union troops later captured him and put him in prison before he was eventually paroled, at which point he did not return to Tocoi, but instead went west to California.

North of Tocoi on the east bank is Solano Point, just east of Solano Cove. It was at Solano Point that famed composer Frederick Delius (1862–1934) arrived in 1884 from his family's textile business in England to try to grow oranges. But instead of growing citrus, he became fascinated by the singing of his black workers, took up music in a serious way, and went on to compose such works as *Florida Suite* (1888); *The Magic Fountain* (1895), an opera about the legendary Fountain of Youth; and

Appalachia, which was used in the movie adaptation of Marjorie Kinnan Rawlings's *The Yearling.* Delius spent relatively little time at Solano Grove (1884–1885 and a short time in 1897), but his work clearly shows the influence of the music he heard

A sign is all that is left at the site where Delius lived near the river.

along the St. Johns. He later gave his property to German conductor Hans Haym, who made Delius's music better known to the public. In 1939, researchers found the four-room frame cottage that Delius had lived in. They moved it in 1961 from Solano Grove to the campus of Jacksonville University, where it serves as the headquarters of the Delius Association. Each year, Jacksonville hosts a Delius Festival to honor the composer.

A little further down the river and situated on a peninsula jutting out from the eastern shore is Picolata, which has had several rebirths depending on who controlled the area. Because the St. Johns narrows appreciably at this point, the Native Americans crossed the river here on the way between the Atlantic coast and Apalachee, which is present-day Tallahassee. Spanish missionaries built a mission there as part of a string of such sites up the St. Johns. The strategic location of the site induced the Spanish to build a fort on each side of the river soon after 1700— Fort Picolata on the eastern shore and Fort San Francisco de Pupo on the western shore. After English colonizer James Oglethorpe of Georgia burned down Fort Picolata in 1740 during his invasion of Florida, the

Spanish rebuilt the fort with a thirty-foot-high tower. British soldiers were garrisoned there during the period of British control of Florida (1763–1783), and Governor James Grant held a conference there in 1765 to establish boundaries with the local Native Americans.

Picolata on the east bank and Bayard Point on the west bank were part of Florida's first federal highway, the Bellamy Road. Two years after the United States acquired Florida from Spain in 1821, the U.S. Congress authorized the building of a road between the two most important towns of the territory: St. Augustine and Pensacola. After surveyor/engineer John Bellamy built the eastern half of the road from Picolata to the Ochlockonee River near Tallahassee, his road helped open up the interior of the territory for settlers.

During the Second Seminole War, a wooden blockhouse was built in Picolata as a supply depot, an Army hospital, and a base of operations in the war against the Native Americans. During the Civil War, Union troops enlarged and occupied the fort. A historical marker at the southeast intersection of SR13 and SR 208 commemorates the site.

In 1875, poet Sidney Lanier visited Picolata and described it as "a place formerly of importance as a landing for passengers, but now . . . only of historic interest." Picolata served as the landing point for steamboats, where a stagecoach would take passengers east to St. Augustine. Tocoi to the south was the landing point for steamboats whose passengers would go by way of the St. Johns Railroad to St. Augustine. In the end, Tocoi superseded the Picolata stop for the steamboats as the railroad connection became more important than the stage connection. A historic marker notes William Bartram's visit to the site.

About a mile north of Picolata, probably around Colee Cove, was the home of John Lee Williams (1775–1856), one of the two men commissioned by the Florida Legislature to select Florida's capital in 1824. Governor DuVal commissioned Williams and Dr. William Simmons to choose a site for a permanent state capital midway between St. Augustine and Pensacola in order to avoid the many problems that legislative delegates experienced in traveling between the two distant cities. Williams wrote two classics of early Florida literature: *A View of West Florida* (1827) and *The Territory of Florida* (1837).

William Tecumseh Sherman (1820–1891), who would later become infamous during his march through Georgia during the Civil War, stayed with John Lee Williams near Colee Cove in 1842 during the Second Seminole War, when he was stationed at Fort Picolata. Sherman later

The long pier at Six Mile Marina allows many boats to tie up. The abandoned boat to the right of the pier has been taken over by weeds.

wrote about the place: "It is a very beautiful spot indeed. Magnificent live oak trees shade the yard, enclosing my splendid quarters, and the St. Johns, a noble sheet of water, about one and a half miles broad, adds beauty to the whole. In fact I would much prefer being here to St. Augustine, for 'tis like being in the country with all the advantages of both town and country, for with a good horse I can ride over at any time in a couple of hours, get books, see the ladies, etc."

Heading north on the river, boaters come to Pacetti Point and then Palmo Cove to the northeast. Flowing into the cove are Mud Alley and Six-Mile Creek. About a mile up Six-Mile Creek is Six Mile Marina, which has the longest private dock we saw on the St. Johns. The Outback Restaurant has a 1500-foot-long floating dock where boats will dock, sometimes five abreast, on weekends, as their owners and passengers enjoy lunch in the restaurant before heading back home by boat. An abandoned boat, complete with a tree growing out of it, adds to the scene near the long dock.

Six-Mile Creek was the site of an alligator attack in 1996, when a fifteen-footer nicknamed Old Tail Light because of the size of his eyes, which seemed to expand at night, lunged at a fiberglass boat carrying a minister out for a fishing trip. As the man later explained, "His head was humongous. He was a monster, as long as my boat, and he was looking right at me." The gator was protecting the carcass of a dead dog he was eating, but the minister in the boat could have been the next meal of the territorial reptile. Rangers warn boaters to leave gators alone, not feed them anything nor swim with pets, and to stay out of the water at dusk and at night, when gators actively feed.

At the northern tip of Palmo Cove is the mouth of Trout Creek, which goes back about three miles. A large marina to the north of the bridge handles small boats, while another one south of the bridge handles larger boats, including sailboats with tall masts.

As we continued north on the river and just before we reached the Shands Bridge, we looked to the right to a point near the base of the bridge. It was there at Smith Point that, according to historian Daniel Schafer of the University of North Florida, William Bartram had his farm. Botanists John Bartram and his son William had visited this area in 1765 on their first trip up the St. Johns. After John returned to Philadelphia, William traveled throughout the Southeast, including up the St.

Shands Bridge connects Green Cove Springs with Picolata and Switzerland on the east shore.

Johns River. He began growing rice and indigo on a small farm where Smith Point is now, but he did not do well. Family friend Henry Laurens (who would later succeed John Hancock as president of the Continental Congress) visited him around 1766 and described William as "Poor Billy

Bartram, a gentle mild young man, no wife, no friend, no companion, no neighbor, no human inhabitant within nine miles of him, the nearest by water, no boat to come to them and these only common soldiers seated on a beggarly spot of land, scant of bare necessities, and totally devoid of the comforts of life, except an inimitable degree of patience, for which he deserves a thousand times better fate."

William would be gone within the year, but he returned in the 1770s, explored much of the St. Johns River, and wrote the significant *Travels Through North & South Carolina, Georgia, East & West Florida* (1791). Interestingly, when William sailed up the St. Johns in 1775 and went past the cove where his farm had been, he made no mention of the site, probably well content to forget about his misguided attempt to wrest a living from the land as a planter. How well he would succeed, though, as a collector of plant specimens and as an observer of wild Florida! North Florida has many plaques noting the William Bartram Trail, indicating just how far-reaching his travels were.

Shands Bridge crosses over from Smith Point to Red Bay Point on the other shore. Because the Shands Bridge is a two-lane span only forty-five feet high, its capacity for vehicular traffic is severely limited, and it doesn't allow larger waterborne vessels to pass underneath. The walls along the bridge are not high, occasionally resulting in cars plunging off the bridge to the river below. This is the only bridge over the St. Johns north of Sanford that does not have a clearance of at least 65 feet, a fact local leaders feel hinders the economic development of Clay County.

The name of the bridge goes back to the man who built it in 1928, A.G. Shands. The wooden bridge at that time was nineteen feet wide and almost two and a half miles long. It carried a lot of traffic until the Depression of the early 1930s, at which time the State Road Department took it over and paid Shands $210,000 for it. By 1959, around 1,700 vehicles were crossing the bridge each day, and so the State Road Department completed a new concrete bridge in 1960.

Green Cove Springs, the large town on the western shore and the county seat of Clay County, takes its name from the sulfur spring near the river. You can walk up to and around the enclosed spring, which used to send out three thousand gallons of sulfur-smelling water a minute into a large pubic swimming pool in a park near the river, and then into the river itself. Today, the output of the spring is half what it used to be—a warning that our aquifer and source of springs is diminishing, probably from overuse over the decades.

The population of the town, which live-oak cutters established in 1830, was 5,378 in the 2000 census. Green Cove Springs was one of the popular wintering places along the river in the 1870s and 1880s, when visitors would swim in the pool and listen to daily band concerts during the winter months. Among the property owners were Gail Borden (who made condensed milk) and J.C. Penney (who founded a chain of popular stores around the country). Penney established Penney Farms six miles to the west for retired religious leaders of all denominations and their spouses. Among the famous local personages was Augusta Savage, an internationally famous sculptor.

The eleven one-thousand-foot-long piers south of Green Cove Springs may seem out of place, but they served a useful purpose between wars. After World War II ended, federal officials developed anchorages there for a mothballed fleet that included as many as three hundred ships. During the Korean War, the Navy reactivated 175 of those ships in what became known as Naval Station Green Cove Springs, but then returned them to the docks after the 1953 truce, where they remained until President Lyndon Johnson sent them to Texas in the 1960s. At that point, the facility closed and Reynolds Aluminum Corporation bought it to develop an industrial park complex, which also uses a former Navy auxiliary air station, Lee Field. Today, the site is called Reynolds Airpark. Now the docks have many different-sized ships and boats tied up as well as in the nearby dry docks.

Just north of the town dock and central park is St. Mary's Episcopal Church, easily seen from the river or by car at 400 St. Johns Avenue. Built in 1879 in the Carpenter Gothic style, the church, which is still used today, was placed on the National Register of Historic Places in 1979. Of particular interest are the small doors below some of the side windows that were used for either ventilation or for escape in case of fire. The church is one of many that were built along the St. Johns in the nineteenth century to cater to winter visitors and to serve as missionary centers. Similar churches can be found in the riverside communities of Enterprise, Crescent City (on Crescent Lake), Federal Point, Hibernia, Mandarin, Orange Park, Arlington, and Fort George Island. The churches, all of which are similar in appearance, resemble churches in

St. Mary's Episcopal Church is in the Carpenter Gothic style.

The spring feeds directly into the public swimming pool.

the northeastern United States rather than the coquina-block structures or so-called "Cracker" frame buildings that one might expect in Florida.

Orangedale, across from Green Cove Springs on the east shore, was the site of a ferry run by Native Americans who had been relocated there by the Spanish from the mission at Mount Royal, which was thirty miles south of Palatka, to the mission San Diego de Salamototo east of Green Cove Springs.

Once we arrived in Green Cove Springs, we were able to tie up at the public dock down from the swimming pool and spend the night at a local bed-and-breakfast. Town officials did not charge us any fee for the docking (take note, Palatka), and we spent an afternoon and night in the pretty little town. The public park/swimming pool right by the river is one of the prettiest along the St. Johns.

ighways 15/17 head north out of Palatka on the western shore. Then SR 209 cuts off to the east, following the sharp turn of the St. Johns, first east, then due north. The highway cuts off to the east four miles north of Palatka and one mile north of Rice Creek (note: the last time I drove on SR 209, it did not have the highway sign). The highway winds around and passes residential areas like Verdiere Point, Bodine Point, Bridgeport, and Ninemile Point, but only occasionally can you see glimpses of the river through the trees. The main highway north (15/17) is preferable for most people, although much of the highway passes through undeveloped land into Green Cove Springs.

by land from Palatka to Green Cove Springs

Just south of Green Cove Springs and near Reynolds Airport, CR 16 cuts off to the east and crosses the St. Johns on the Shands Bridge. Between the bridge and the town of Green Cove Springs are eleven piers, two of which are private and the rest commercial. When I visited there in 2004, the two private piers had four hundred boats either docking there or in dry dock or in storage, with another fifty boats on the waiting list. Visitors are free to wander along the two piers and chat with boat owners, many of whom are busy scraping, painting, or repairing their vessels.

On the east side of the river, SR 207 goes through East Palatka. Highway 207A goes close to the river, but the many houses there block out the view of the St. Johns up to Federal Point. Highway 207 goes north-northeast through Hastings and its potato farms until it reaches Spud, after which SR 13, the William Bartram Scenic Highway, cuts off and goes northwest along the river to Shands Bridge. SR 13 passes through small towns like Racy Point, Riverdale, Tocoi, Lane Landing, Meldrim Park, and Picolata, offering some very beautiful views of the river. If you have to choose a land trip from Palatka to Green Cove Springs and you have the time, take this route. It far surpasses in beauty and history the trip on the western side of the river.

One mile north of Tocoi is a sign marking the place where composer Frederick Delius lived in 1884–1885; his house is now on the campus of Jacksonville University farther to the north. A short distance north of the original site is the Solano Cove Wildlife Management Group. A plaque on the east side of the road at Highway 208 indicates that Fort Picolata is the site where John and William Bartram witnessed the signing of a peace treaty with the Native Americans in 1765, during the British occupation

A gate bars the entrance to Solano Cove.

of Florida. 4.2 miles north of Picolata is a bridge over Six-Mile Creek, from which one can see a long pier.

Green Cove Springs is a very pleasant town where we were able to catch our breath before reaching the busyness of the rest of the river and its increasingly crowded sites that would bring us back into the twenty-first century. While there, we could easily understand how tourists arriving by steamboat in the nineteenth century from Jacksonville and the colder North would luxuriate in its public pool and natural charm. Each time I have visited the town, I have been pleasantly surprised by how charming it is, especially near the river.

7 Magnolia Springs to Mandarin and Orange Park

For ourselves, we are getting reconciled to a sort of tumble-down, wild, picnicky kind of life,—this general happy-go-luckiness which Florida inculcates. If we painted her, we should not represent her as a neat, trim damsel, with starched linen cuffs and collar; she would be a brunette, dark but comely, with gorgeous tissues, a general disarray and dazzle, and with a sort of jolly untidiness, free, easy, and joyous.

—*Harriet Beecher Stowe,*
Palmetto Leaves *(1873)*

by water from Magnolia Springs to Mandarin and Orange Park

This is the last section of our trip that will be relatively uncongested before we reach Jacksonville and head over to Mayport near the Atlantic Ocean. Even so, we notice how the traffic begins to increase, to some degree on the river, but most definitely on the land. As the metropolitan center of Jacksonville continues to increase in size, more and more of those who work there are choosing to live in distant suburbs along the St. Johns and around nearby lakes, such as the towns of Orange Park, Ortega, and Avondale on the west side of the river, and Mandarin, Englewood, and Arlington on the east side.

The water north of Green Cove Springs has a small amount of salinity, less than one part per thousand. While geologists would expect the upper parts of the St. Johns to be less salty, the major springs that pour into the St. Johns above Sanford give it a salinity and mineral feature that accommodate many different kinds of fish, including saltwater species that make their way far up the river. Environmentalist Archie Carr points out in *A Naturalist in Florida: A Celebration of Eden* that parts of the river must have been coastal lagoons eons ago, just as the Halifax River, Indian River, and Mosquito Lagoon are today—that is, estuaries with direct connection to the ocean. As sea levels fell during the ice ages, the lagoons associated with the St. Johns were disconnected from the ocean and the north-flowing river that drained much of Central Florida.

Today, the St. Johns harbors about 170 species of fish, of which some 55 are freshwater and many are adapted to both fresh and salt water. A process called *osmoregulation* allows the fish to adapt to fresh or salt water. Bob Wattendorf of the Division of Fisheries explains in an article that "in fresh water, to counteract the physical phenomenon that forces water into their bodies, fish kidneys produce vast quantities of low-salt urine. Freshwater fish eliminate 10 percent of their body weight daily as urine." If they did not eliminate that urine, it could seriously harm them. The American shad is an example of a fish that is adapted to both fresh and salt water. It returns from the Atlantic Ocean to the St. Johns each winter to spawn. The young fish then swim to the ocean and mature; then they return to the river to spawn.

The town of Magnolia Springs right above Green Cove Springs takes its name from its own local spring, which was a popular resort in the

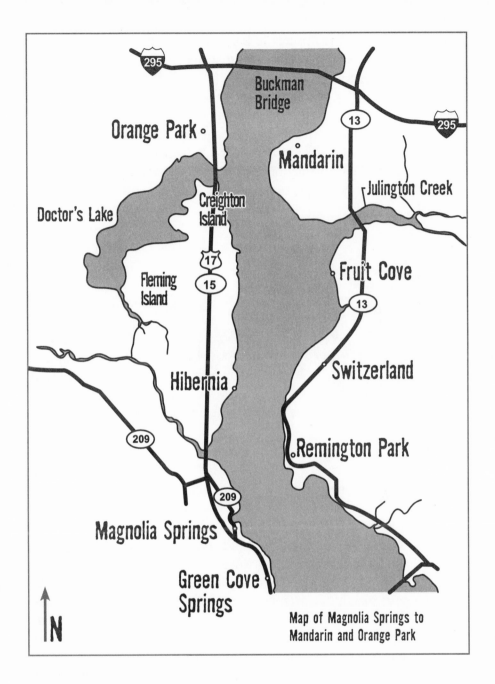

Map of Magnolia Springs to
Mandarin and Orange Park

nineteenth century. One of the guests there was President Grover Cleveland, who apparently liked the spring water from there so much that he had bottles of it sent to the White House while he was president.

Just above Magnolia Springs is Black Creek, a name that curiously comes from a corruption of the Spanish name *Río Blanco* or "White River." "Black" seems more appropriate because of the darkness of the water caused—not by pollution—but by the debris from the many trees along its shores.

In 1990, the St. Johns River Water Management District bought over six thousand acres along the North Fork of Black Creek, and then three years later the Nature Conservancy bought another five thousand acres, with the result that eighty-five percent of Upper Black Creek's pristine woods and wetlands is protected for the foreseeable future. That is particularly important for the St. Johns because the inevitable expansion of Middleburg and Orange Park could have degraded the creek and eventually the river. The protected area is home to the Black Creek crayfish (found nowhere else), the blue butterwort, hooded pitcher plant, gopher tortoise, and fox squirrel. The crayfish, also called crawfish or crawdad, is closely related to the lobster and usually lives in fresh water, although a few can survive in salt water. The butterwort, a carnivorous plant that enjoys several hours of sunlight each day, thrives in acid soil. The hooded pitcher plant, which attracts bees, butterflies, and birds, needs consistently moist soil. The gopher tortoise builds vast burrows in the sandy soil, where many other species can be found as "squatters." This tortoise is extremely important to the health of the entire ecosystem. The fox squirrel can be black, gray, or mostly white and often has a black nose. The Florida Division of Forestry manages the area as a state forest.

Magnolia Springs Hotel in Magnolia Springs, Florida.

The next town up the western shore is Hibernia, a community and old plantation house on Fleming Island. The island is named after the Fleming Family, which developed a cotton plantation there from a Spanish grant in the 1790s. The Flemings had come from Ireland and called the settlement Hibernia after the poetical name for Ireland. The mansion they built on the island escaped damage during the Civil War and lasted into the mid-1900s, but eventually deteriorated. Builders used the bricks from the seven chimneys of the original mansion as part of a new dwelling on the site.

The town of Hibernia still has a Gothic-style church that dates back to the nineteenth century. Margaret Seton Fleming Biddle, a resident of Hibernia in the early 1800s, wrote that "at this time there was one road—little more than a cart track—deep in sand and solitude, to the inland town of Middleburg. . . . The St. John's [sic] was the great highway of all that part of the country, the Main Street of Florida. Each plantation had its own eight-oar barge, manned by strong slaves, as a means of transportation on the river." As we boated near Hibernia, we noticed how the river narrowed considerably before opening once again near Julington Creek. The depth of the St. Johns remained relatively deep in the middle, averaging between fifteen and twenty-three feet, but the speed of the river definitely increased. We had a straight shot north to the beckoning city of Jacksonville, but we still didn't have the heavy boat traffic we might have expected.

Up a little ways is Ragged Point on the west shore of the St. Johns. Moccasin Slough, which belongs to Clay County, sits there along the river, with its 260 acres of valuable land that will remain untouched by developers. The recreational park and nature preserve are part of the Black Creek Bicycle Trail, a five-mile-long trail in Clay County. Moccasin Slough was purchased with the help of the Trust for Public Land, a national nonprofit group dedicated to the protection and conservation of land for the public good.

Farther up on the western bank is Creighton Island, which was owned by John Creighton in the early 1800s. Moving on, we go under the Highway 15/17 bridge into Doctor's Inlet, then Doctor's Lake, past Doctors Lake Marina. The name Doctor's Inlet is found on maps dating back to the British occupation of Florida (1763–1783). The lake, which extends to the southwest for about four miles, is lined with large homes and long docks. We stopped along the northern shore at the North Council Aquatic Camp, where dozens of youngsters were attending summer camp. Boaters need to be careful near the northern shore because of submerged piles and at least one wreck that our nautical map indicated. There were canoes and sailboats around the lake, which had a depth of eight to ten feet in much of the middle of the body of water. As we headed out into the river, we could notice the increase in boat traffic, not only from such coves as Doctor's Lake and Julington Creek, but also from the boats heading south from Jacksonville.

The Highway 17 bridge over Doctor's Lake has a clearance of thirty-seven feet. Boaters seeking refuge from strong winds can find inlets in the lake where they can take cover. Many such inlets along the St. Johns, especially around Jacksonville, are often lit up gaily around Christmastime as people festoon their waterfront homes and boats.

Boaters traveling in the Jacksonville area should monitor the VHF weather channel, especially channel #1, in order to hear of any approaching storms. From Palatka south, channel #2 from Melbourne or channel #3 from Gainesville can usually be picked up.

North of Doctor's Lake is Orange Park, one of the major suburbs of Jacksonville on the west bank of the St. Johns. The name of the community, which was established in 1876, refers to the orange groves that existed there in the nineteenth century but were wiped out by freezes.

The original name of Orange Park was Laurel Grove, which took its name from a plantation owned by Zephaniah Kingsley. Kingsley (1765–1843) was a Scot who married an African princess, Anna Madgigaine Jai, and set up several plantations on the St. Johns. Throughout his life, although he wrote about the evils of slavery and promoted the fair treatment of slaves, he relied on slaves to amass his wealth. Acquiring slaves from African chiefs, he trained them to become field hands and skilled laborers to make them more valuable and then either used them on his own plantations or smuggled them into the United States across the St. Marys River from his plantation on the St. Johns at a time when the Spanish controlled Florida.

In 1812, Kingsley became involved in what was called the Patriot War, an attempt by expansionists in the United States to take over Florida, which the Spanish still controlled. They also wanted to disarm freed African Americans who had become part of the Free Black Militia of East Florida. The Patriots went to Laurel Grove, captured Kingsley, and took him to Cowford, where he was induced to support the rebels. He hosted a legislative council at Laurel Grove in July of 1812, which set as its goal acquiring the East Florida Territory and giving it to the United States. President James Madison, however, withdrew official support from the Patriots when the public expressed its disapproval of the tactics they used in Florida, for example the seizure of Fernandina. At that point,

Historic riverfront property in Switzerland

the Native Americans, who were not really a part of the Patriot War but who were intent on driving out the whites, joined with their African American allies, attacked Laurel Grove, captured the slaves there, and burned down the buildings. Kingsley would later concentrate his energies on his plantation, moving it to Fort George Island (see chapter nine). Today, the names of Kingsley Avenue and Kingsley Village are about the only remnants of Laurel Grove in Orange Park.

On the eastern shore of the St. Johns above the Shands Bridge is Remington Park, named by English colonists after a family in the 1890s. The next town up the eastern shore is Switzerland, named by Francis Fatio, who settled there during the British occupation of Florida (1763–1783) and transplanted the name of his native Switzerland. Some of the street names near the river (Geneva, Matterhorn, and Swiss Oaks Court) continue the Swiss theme.

As we enter the Duval County/Jacksonville area, we pass Julington Creek to the east, of which Harriet Beecher Stowe wrote in *Palmetto Leaves:* "But now we are at the mouth of Julington, and running across to a point of land on the other side. Our boat comes to anchor under a grove of magnolia trees which lean over the water. They are not yet fully in blossom. One lily-white bud and one full-blown flower appear on a low branch overhanging the river, and are marked to be gathered when we return. We go up, and begin strolling along the shore. The magnolia-grove extends along the edge of the water for half a mile." Such vivid descriptions of northern Florida, which she wrote about to her friends back in the cold of New England, attracted many tourists to this part of the state in the late nineteenth century.

Even today, Julington Creek and its tributary, Durbin Creek, have stretches of unspoiled land on either side. They become narrower as they go back away from the river. The William Bartram Canoe Trail begins on Durbin Creek in a wetland and proceeds three miles under an overhang of cypress trees. After the creek goes under Racetrack Road, it widens before joining Corklan Creek, then Julington, and finally the St. Johns. Canoers should put in south of Racetrack Road, west of I-95. The distance from Durbin Creek to Julington Creek is 8.5 miles. The Highway 13 Bridge over Julington has a clearance of about fifteen feet; water depths can be only five feet at low water. The worst hazard is motorboats on Julington, but boaters need to watch for low tree limbs, submerged piles, and jagged rocks.

We docked at Clark's Fish Camp and were able to have lunch indoors.

We boated up Julington Creek to Clark's Fish Camp at 12903 Hood Landing Road. The facility, which is really a restaurant and not a fish camp, is unusual because of the dozens of stuffed animals and hundreds of mounted fish on the walls. The propri-

etor makes it clear that the owners did not kill any of the animals, but that the animals, especially the African ones, died of old age or illness while in captivity. The facility began as a one-building fish camp at Hood Landing in the mid-1970s, but has evolved into a very popular restaurant. When we were there, the restaurant did not have any sign on the riverside, but lots of boaters clearly knew where it is.

Near Julington Creek is where the Confederates sank the *Maple Leaf* steamer in 1864. The vessel was 173 feet long and 24 feet wide and had a depth of almost eleven feet. After the Civil War began, the federal government chartered the double-stacked, side-wheel steamer to transport army troops. In the spring of 1864, Union troops loaded her with four hundred tons of baggage for a trip to Jacksonville from Charleston, South Carolina.

When the Maple Leaf reached Jacksonville and before troops could unload the boat, local authorities sent her with ninety cavalrymen and their horses sixty miles south to Palatka. After unloading the cavalrymen and horses in Palatka and picking up three Confederate prisoners and some Union sympathizers fleeing the area, the boat headed back toward Jacksonville.

Meanwhile Confederate troops were placing beer-keg mines, each with seventy pounds of explosive powder, in the St. Johns near Mandarin Point twelve miles south of Jacksonville. On April 1, 1864, the *Maple Leaf* hit one of the mines and exploded, killing four deck hands who had been sleeping near the ship's bow. The other passengers survived and made their way to shore. Within seven minutes the vessel sank to a depth of twenty feet.

As time went on, the ship settled into the mud at the bottom of the river, until, eventually, seven feet of oxygen-lacking mud covered the wreck. This made the vessel almost impossible to find but preserved the tons of goods on the vessel. In the 1980s, Jacksonville dentist and part–time archaeologist Keith Holland, the great-great-grandson of an Alabama Confederate soldier, began doing library research to discover exactly where the boat lay. He had some idea of its location, but needed to pinpoint the site with dives. With his own money, grants from state organizations, and the approval of state and federal agencies, Dr. Holland formed St. Johns Archaeological Expeditions, Inc., which included historians, divers, engineers, and admiralty lawyers. Diving and finding objects on the river bottom must have been next to impossible because of the river's brackishness. Nonetheless, Holland and other divers discovered the exact location of the wreck and retrieved over one thousand pounds from the sunken wreck. The artifacts found included porcelain dishes, sewing utensils, even repair kits to fix worn-out shoes and clothing, indicating what ordinary soldiers carried during the Civil War. Many of the artifacts recovered are in local museums. In 1994, officials named the shipwreck site of the *Maple Leaf* a National Historical Landmark. But most of the wreck's four hundred tons still lies at the bottom of the river in what might be considered a sealed time capsule.

Beyond Julington Creek is Mandarin, a place with several names in its history: San Antonia when Spain controlled Florida, St. Anthony under British rule, Monroe when the United States took control of the territory in 1821, and Mandarin in 1841 when Ebenezar Eveleth, a traveler from Asia, settled there (mandarin is a variety of orange from China).

Harriet Beecher Stowe (1811–1896), author of *Uncle Tom's Cabin* (1851), spent her winters in Mandarin with her minister husband from 1868 until 1884. Her letters back home to the cold Northeast, letters which were later published as *Palmetto Leaves,* praised the land and weather and people so highly that thousands of tourists were drawn to the Sunshine State. In her book, *Mandarin on the St. Johns,* Mary Graff recounts the story of Stowe's visit to her brother in Tallahassee. She feared an unfeeling welcome by Floridians who might have believed, as President Abraham Lincoln once did, that she was the "little lady who hastened the Civil War." However,

The Mandarin Community Club is on the site where the Stowes used to live.

people in Tallahassee received her kindly and graciously. Graff also tells how, when the Stowes lived in their house on the St. Johns, one of the local steamboats that ran boats between Jacksonville and Mandarin assured the passengers of a view of America's most famous woman author. After a particularly rude woman had walked onto the grounds of the Stowe house and up onto the porch, she met Calvin Stowe and had the nerve to say: "But I would have preferred to meet Mrs. Stowe." "So had I, Madam," Reverend Stowe retorted. "So had I—a thousand times."

My favorite anecdote about Harriet Beecher Stowe and Mandarin was a question she raised after a description of the beautiful Florida weather: "I never knew such altogether perfect weather. It is enough to make a saint out of the toughest old Calvinist that ever set his face as a flint. How do you think New England theology would have fared, if our fathers had been landed here instead of on Plymouth Rock?" Today, Mandarin is a suburb of Jacksonville but still retains the charm that attracted the Stowes, including the majestic live oaks that form a five-mile-long canopy arching over Mandarin Road. One can see from the location of the town why Timucuan Indians settled on its bluff centuries ago.

by land from Magnolia Springs to Mandarin and Orange Park

North of Magnolia on US 17 at the intersection with Raggedy Point Road, signs indicate the location of Moccasin Slough, which extends out to the river. This is a wildlife refuge in Clay County with over three thousand feet of frontage along the St. Johns River, the only designated American Heritage River in the Southeastern United States. The park will remain the habitat for several threatened and endangered species of waterfowl as well as for the American alligator. The Trust for Public Land, a national nonprofit entity dedicated to the protection and conservation of land for the public good, helped buy the property with monetary help from the Florida Communities Trust, Florida Department of Environmental Protection, Clay County, and the land's former owners.

On the east shore of the river, SR 13 (San Jose Boulevard) follows the flow of the St. Johns north to Jacksonville through towns such as Orangedale, Remington Park, Switzerland, Fruit Cove, and Mandarin. A little inland from the river near Switzerland is Beluthahatchee Lake, named after an Indian word meaning "Nirvana on Water." The twenty-

The church of Our Saviour in Mandarin is right next to the river.

acre lake is part of a seventy-acre spread where one of Florida's most important living writers has resided for several decades. Stetson Kennedy, born in 1916, has written about Florida and the Ku Klux Klan (see Further Reading for details). In the 1930s, he worked on the *Florida Guide,* a WPA Writers Project, with such writers as Carita Doggett Corse and Zora Neale Hurston.

When I visited Kennedy at Lake Dwellers, his home on Beluthahatchee Lake, he told me how the Klan once invaded his house while he was away. Instead of burning all of his papers, many of which were exposés of the Klan, the intruders threw them into the lake. When he returned and found the stolen papers all over the lake, he spent weeks retrieving them and laying them all over his yard to dry.

Harriet Beecher Stowe's winter home in Mandarin, which used to be on Mandarin Road near where the Community Center stands today, is no longer there. A historical marker in front of the Community Center notes the purchase by Harriet Beecher Stowe and her husband of their home on the banks of the St. Johns on land that was part of the Fairbanks Grant, one of the original land grants from the British government. Apparently their son Charles, believing that his parents had not been treated as well as they should have in Mandarin, had their house torn down in 1916 and offered the lumber to anyone who would carry it away. The chapel wing of the Episcopal Church of Our Saviour at 12236 Mandarin Road is a replica of the church that Stowe and her husband helped establish in Mandarin in 1883, but which Hurricane Dora destroyed in 1964.

Just north of Mandarin, driving is much slower as the traffic becomes congested by Highway 295, which circles Jacksonville. The Buckman Bridge beyond Mandarin leads over to Orange Park on the west shore.

8 Jacksonville

Our position is now an advanced one; popular and elegant lines of steamers connect us with Savannah and Charleston; we are tapping the St. Johns River, its lakes and tributaries, with results as golden as the fruit they supply.

—Florida Union *newspaper,*
March 10, 1874

by water from Orange Park through Jacksonville

Jacksonville has had a long love/hate relationship with the St. Johns. Supposedly, the Timucuan Indians called the river *wacca pilatka* "place where cows cross," although they had never seen cows before the Spanish arrived in the sixteenth century; and the depth of the water and the speed of the current there would make it difficult for cows. The narrowness of the waterway has to be the reason behind the name. *Wacca* in fact sounds too close to the Spanish *vaca* "cow" to be coincidental. The Spanish called this part of the river Pass of San Nicolas because Fort San Nicholas was nearby, possibly where the county courthouse is today on Liberty Street.

When the British controlled the area (1763–1783), they established a ferry crossing to the north bank at Cow Ford, with one branch of the so-called King's Road heading west to Apalachee country, and the other branch heading northwest to St. Marys River on the Georgia border. After the territory became part of the United States in 1821, the name became Jacksonville to honor General Andrew Jackson, the first territorial governor of Florida, but a man who never actually visited the city. However, after Jackson became President of the United States, he did help his namesake town by naming it an official port of entry to Florida, a designation that brought business and money into Jacksonville. Documents detailing exactly when the city officially came into being in June 1822 have not been found, so the city celebrates its birthday on June 15, the date when settlers there petitioned U.S. Congress for recognition as a port of entry.

The independent attitude of many early Jacksonville residents extended to their reluctance to pay taxes. That attitude resulted in a decided vote against Florida's becoming a state in 1845: thirty-one for statehood, but 174 against it. Fortunately, residents in the rest of the territory voted for it, and Florida became the twenty-seventh state in the Union.

During the American Civil War, Union troops occupied Jacksonville four different times, but the city survived that and Reconstruction to find itself what some called "The Winter Capital" of the country at the end of the nineteenth century. The influx of winter tourists and the praise bestowed on the city by such writers as Harriet Beecher Stowe and Sidney Lanier led to the building of large hotels to accommodate the many visitors.

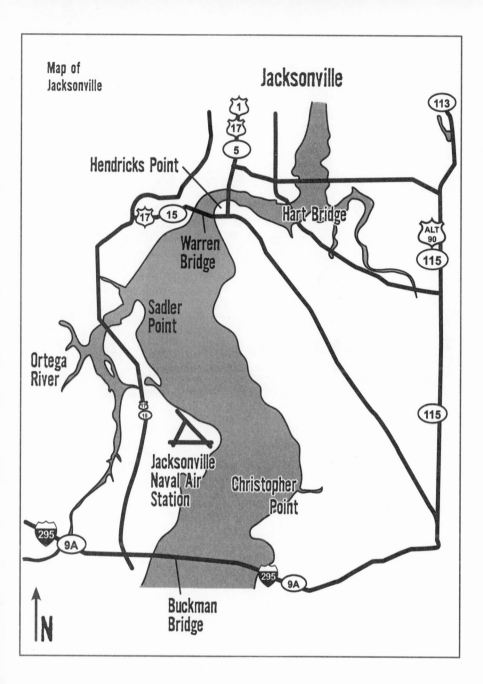

Map of Jacksonville

Jacksonville

A devastating fire in 1901 destroyed many of those hotels as well as much of the downtown area, but officials were able to use the tragedy to rebuild the city, especially with such skilled architects as Henry John Klutho. The new city was geared less to tourists than to businessmen,

St. James Hotel after

Jacksonville's St.
James Hotel after
the fire of 1901.

who designated the city as The Gateway City to a booming Florida. The railroad that Henry Flagler built in the early twentieth century, the one that went to St. Augustine, the Palm Beaches, Miami, and Key West, ended Jacksonville's claim as a winter resort as sun-seekers headed south from the cold of North Florida.

Jacksonville is definitely the city that the St. Johns River has influenced more than any other in Florida. Much of Florida's history in the nineteenth century was involved with this metropolis, primarily because its location in the northeastern part of the state and on the major river entrance to central Florida made it the entrance port for thousands of immigrants, temporary and permanent, to the state.

Several important factors have fueled Jacksonville's growth: its strategic position on the river, its inland location away from the hurricanes that battered the coast, its deep-harbor facilities, and its railroad connections. The fact that it had connections to the rest of the world through its ocean port and to the rest of the country through its railroad connections helped it thrive as a commercial center.

The steamboat era on the St. Johns, from the 1820s to the 1920s, saw around three hundred vessels plying the waters and carrying passengers and cargo to inland sites long before roads and rail lines opened up the state. From the 1870s on, sickly visitors traveled on the river to Florida springs, especially Silver Springs, in hopes of relief from various ailments or at least for some warmth from the harsh Northern winters. Hunting and fishing enthusiasts also used the steamboats to reach formerly inaccessible places where they could find much prey.

The steamboats had another use too. Because communication in the nineteenth century was erratic at best, the boats that left Jacksonville for an upriver run could be used to warn of an approaching hard freeze. Some of the steamboats would hoist a white flag with a black square in the center or would use different whistle blasts to warn the farmers along the river, even varying the blasts to indicate what type of freeze to expect.

The reliability of the steamboats, which could pretty much run on schedule despite head winds, rough weather, or changing tides, helped those who lived along the river. The building of larger vessels, made possible because of the increasing use of iron and steel in the boats, allowed them to carry

Many types of boats ply the river around Jacksonville. This one is reminiscent of the steamboat days.

larger cargoes and more passengers, and the mail. The increasing size of the boats meant that towns along the river had to build longer docks into the St. Johns and to dredge as best they could to accommodate the deeper drafts. Some of the pilings of those long docks can still be seen along the river. Edward Mueller's *St. Johns River Steamboats* describes the many types of vessels—side wheeler, stern wheel, and propeller-driven boats—that used to navigate the St. Johns.

As we passed through Jacksonville, we were surprised at the lack of boat traffic. True, we did go through on a weekday, but—apart from the water taxis that shuttled people back and forth across the river and an occasional party boat—there really was not much traffic. That would not be true in the last section of our trip, from above Jacksonville to Mayport. Jacksonville has done a good job of keeping freighters and cargo ships north of the downtown area and confined to the industrial parks along Heckscher Drive.

Just above Orange Park, we went under the six-lane Buckman/I-295 Bridge, the one that takes traffic from the very busy I-95 and circles it around Jacksonville. Just north of the bridge on the west side is the Jacksonville Rudder Club. Among its annual events is the Mug Race, a one-day sailboat race from Palatka to the Rudder Club. The race, which began over fifty years ago and is usually held on the first weekend of May, claims to be the longest river sailboat race in the world, covering forty-two miles down the river. As many as four hundred boats participate.

On the west side, just after the Buckman/I-295 Bridge, we pass the Jacksonville Naval Air Station and watch as planes practice taking off and landing on two of the runways. The personnel at the air station are involved in anti-submarine warfare training involving helicopters and planes such as the P3 Orions. Boaters may even see the strange sight of a helicopter hovering over the river, putting its sound-detection sonar into the water to practice the art of discovering vessels beneath the surface. Civilian boaters may find such planes dipping the sonars behind and in front of their boats in order to practice recognizing the signals emitted by different vessels. Boaters at night may be surprised at the bright blip on their radar screens caused by helicopters in the area. The turbo-prop Orions make frequent touch-and-go landings on the naval station's runways and go around and around the area on practice runs.

The salaries paid to the approximately ten thousand military and seven thousand civilians who work there at any given time have had a very strong impact on the economy of the area. In 1907, local officials bought three hundred acres at Black Point, which is at the first sharp point north of the 295 bridge, and gave them to the state to build a troop-training site, Camp Joseph E. Johnston. Another thousand acres were acquired over the next few years . Troops also trained there during World War I. When federal officials complained that too many of the soldiers stationed there were getting drunk, voters went to the polls and made the county "dry." During World War II, voters approved a $1.1 million bond issue to pay for more land around Black Point, which became the Jacksonville Naval Air Station. Some of that bond money was also used to pay for land in Mayport that would become the Mayport Naval Station.

Behind the Naval Air Station and emptying into the St. Johns is the large Ortega River, formerly known as McGirts Creek. Daniel McGirt (who may have spelled his last name with a second *t*) was a soldier who fought for the Americans in the Carolinas during the Revolutionary War, but who fled south after an argument with his commanding officer about a horse. In Florida, McGirt joined the British East Florida Rangers and led raids through Georgia. After the war, he settled down in what is now Ortega, south of Jacksonville, where he stole cattle and slaves from everyone he could. The British captured him right before they ceded East Florida to Spain in 1783 and sent him to the Bahamas. He somehow managed to return to Florida, where he resumed his illicit activities. In 1785, McGirt was arrested and sent to Havana. After the Spanish released him, he made his way back to Florida, but was arrested and deported. He settled in the Bahamas and then South Carolina, where he died. McGirts Point (now known as Sadler Point) as well as McGirts Boulevard (which parallels the Ortega River down to US 17) commemorate the outlaw.

The area surrounding the Ortega River was once owned by one of the so-called rebels of nineteenth-century Florida: John McIntosh, who proclaimed himself the president of the Republic of East Florida. He established the Republic, which lasted from 1812 to 1816, in an effort to induce the United States to push the Spanish out of Florida and annex it— which eventually happened, but not as quickly as the rebels had hoped. Various rebel groups took control of Fernandina above the St. Johns River, showing how ineffective Spanish rule was in the area. However, it would be several years before the United States took over Florida, but the rebels at least paved the way for that annexation. Sadler Point on the west shore honors a son-in-law of McIntosh.

The Ortega River has boatyards and yachting facilities on the north shore and expensive homes on the south shore. The bascule bridge near the entrance to the river has a clearance of about nine feet, while the railway bascule bridge further on has a clearance of only two feet. The Highway 134 bridge has a clearance of twenty feet and leads to several miles of relatively undisturbed scenery, which is unusual since this is so close to Jacksonville. Before that point, many marine-related businesses make their home along the Ortega.

The large buildings on the west between Ortega and the Fuller Warren Bridge are part of various hospitals there: Doctors Hospital, St. Vincent's Hospital, and Riverside Hospital. Jacksonville has been able to attract some major medical facilities such as the Mayo Clinic, Joslin Diabetes Clinic, University Medical Center, and a branch of Shands Hospital of the University of Florida.

Directly across from the Naval Air Station and in the San Jose part of Jacksonville on the east bank is one of the most famous private college-preparatory schools in North Florida: the Bolles School. Founded in 1933 as an all-boys military school spread across fifty-two acres, the school dropped its military status and, in 1971, began admitting girls.

As the river doglegs dramatically to the east before going under three bridges, it narrows considerably, becoming deeper and more rapid before heading north again at Empire Point. The three bridges at the center of Jacksonville that cross the river are, from south to northeast: the Fuller Warren Bridge (named after a former Jacksonville city councilman, county representative in the state legislature, and governor of Florida from 1949 to 1953); the Acosta Bridge (named for St. Elmo W. "Chic" Acosta, who had served Duval County as a state representative and county commissioner); and the Main Street Bridge.

The Fuller Warren Bridge opened in 1954 and served the community well for over forty years, but it deteriorated and was finally replaced in 2002. The new bridge, which retains its original name, has three lanes in each direction and carries over 100,000 vehicles a day. The main span over the river stretches 250 feet and has a vertical clearance of seventy-five feet. The original Acosta Bridge, which was called the St. Johns River Bridge, was built over the river in 1919–1920. It was the first vehicular bridge over the St. Johns in Jacksonville, and it had a lower span for the railroad. The new Acosta Bridge, which was built in the 1990s, has a vertical clearance of seventy-five feet and carries over 40,000 vehicles a day. The Main Street Bridge was built in the late 1930s to carry US 1 over the St. Johns. The 365-foot-long

The Landing is one of the most popular eating and shopping places in Jacksonville.

continuous truss vertical lift-span at the center of the bridge is the longest in Florida.

A little beyond the three bridges is the Isaiah D. Hart Bridge, which was named for the city's founder and leader of the settlers of Cow Ford who laid out the city in 1822. It opened to the public in 1967. The bridge, which has a clearance of 135 feet, comes out on the western bank where the Alltel Stadium hosts football games such as the Gator Bowl. The Wolfson Baseball Park Complex is nearby. The moving of the port facilities from this area to Talleyrand after World War II allowed officials to build the beautiful Metropolitan Park at the site of abandoned docks between the Main Street Bridge and Isaiah Hart Bridge.

The Hart and Main Street Bridges are used during the annual spring-time Gate River Run, a 9.3-mile (15 kilometer) run that attracts as many as eight thousand runners. Sponsors bill it as "the largest participation-sporting event in Jacksonville."

In the downtown Jacksonville area, you can see the Jacksonville Landing shopping and dining complex on the north bank between the Acosta and Main Street Bridges. Just east of the Main Street Bridge, you can see the 1.2-mile-long Riverwalk on the south bank connecting the Museum of Science and History with the Jacksonville Historical Center.

Commodore Point at the western tip of the Isaiah Hart Bridge played a role in one of the most infamous shipwrecks in Florida history. When Stephen Crane, author of *The Red Badge of Courage* (1895), left on a ship called *Commodore* in 1896 to cover an insurrection in Cuba for a newspaper, the ship struck a sandbar at Commodore Point and later ran aground near Mayport, but the captain failed to have divers check for damage to the hull and proceeded on his way to the open ocean. About eighteen miles off Mosquito Inlet east of Daytona Beach, the heavy pounding from waves weakened her further and she sprang a leak. Most of the crew scrambled into lifeboats and made it to safety, after which Crane wrote one of America's most famous short stories, "The Open Boat."

Across from Commodore Point lie the Arlington River and Pottsburg Creek on the eastern shore. Many people live along these waterways, but new boaters to the area should mind their charts carefully since the mouth of the Arlington can be very shallow. Also, a strong tidal range here can cause havoc to boats that are not anchored well.

After Commodore Point, the river turns to the north and goes under the John E. Mathews Bridge, which commemorates a former member of the Florida House of Representatives and later chief justice of the Florida Supreme Court who promoted the building of bridges at Jacksonville while he was in the legislature. The bridge was built in 1953, is 7,375 feet long, and has a vertical clearance of 149.5 feet.

Off on the east bank in the Arlington section is Jacksonville University, a private school with about thirty buildings on 214 acres. Its 2,000-plus students come from some forty states and forty foreign countries. The university is the site of the Frederick Delius House, which was moved there from Solano Grove in 1961. Delius was an English immigrant who discovered a great talent for composing music while living near the St. Johns (see chapter six for more). The university has an extensive collection of notes and papers associated with Delius. The Delius Music Festival each spring attracts many music lovers to its campus.

Across the river on the west side is the Jacksonville Port Authority, Talleyrand Docks and Terminals. The main port used to be closer to downtown Jacksonville, but after World War II officials moved the main port to Talleyrand, which allowed developers to beautify the river's banks upstream and kept much of the city's industrial complex to the north, away from downtown and closer to the mouth of the river.

North of there, just before the river turns due east and heads for Mayport is the confluence of the Trout River from the west. The U.S. Navy Fuel Depot is at the point where the Trout River meets the St. Johns.

The St. Johns has been under the threat of pollution for the past two hundred years, whether from farmers using fertilizers which eventually reached the river, or engineers beginning a Cross–Florida Barge Canal (which would have drastically affected the flow of water west of the river), or industries pumping waste into the river before regulations curtailed that, or even homeowners dowsing their lawns with pesticides that eventually make their way to the river.

Maintenance of the river is often a double-edged sword. For example, the Army Corps of Engineers periodically dredges to maintain a channel deep enough for vessels such as fuel barges. But this disturbs the pollutants that lie in the muck at the bottom, sending them out to harm shellfish and grasses. The abundant use of fertilizers on farms can seriously damage the river, as occurred in the killing of Lake Apopka to the south. Even the discharge of storm water runoff into the river from the towns along the way, while providing an inexpensive way for officials to get rid of the unwanted water, has led to the degradation of the river.

Optimists have some reason for hope. They can point to the increased monitoring by scientists with the St. Johns River Water Management District, by watchdogs from groups like the Riverkeepers, and by homeowners and fishermen who complain to officials about deteriorating conditions along the river.

Geography also provides an unexpected benefit in that the river runs through only one state. Consider the situation of the Apalachicola River to the west. Floridians trying to protect their section of that waterway, particularly oysters growers in Apalachicola Bay, are under constant onslaught from those who live out of state. People in Georgia want to siphon off much of its water flow to satisfy the growing needs of a thirsty Atlanta, and farmers in Alabama want to use the river to irrigate the many farms along the river. At least those trying to maintain the quality of the St. Johns do not have to try to reach a compromise with officials from three states.

Pollution from the industrial parks north of Jacksonville has seeped toward the south, even though the river flows north, especially due to the tidal flows that reach down to Lake George. Floridians are finally becoming aware of how fragile the river is. We have come a long way from the days when developers could do whatever they wanted with the land and river. Future generations will greatly benefit from today's stricter laws, but there is much more to be done to protect the river and the life along and within it.

by land from Orange Park through Jacksonville

This land section of the trip is the most congested of the whole trip down the St. Johns. On the west side of the river, US 17 goes north from Orange Park through the city to Heckscher Drive, which then runs along the northern side of the river.

For the other side of the river, cross the I-295 bridge (Buckman Bridge) above Orange Park and head for the river north of the city. My own favorite route, unless I want to see something in the city itself, is to take I-295 to I-95, north to road 115, right on Atlantic Boulevard, then north on Monument Road to Fort Caroline National Monument.

9 Mayport

The early sun was a hot copper plate in an opal-flecked sky as the ship made the mouth of the St. Johns River and began beating his way up the tortuous channel which twisted and writhed through the marsh and sandy flats to the town twenty miles upstream.

—*Robert Wilder,* God Has a Long Face

by water from Jacksonville to Mayport

The final stretch of the river is in some ways the most interesting from a historical and commercial point of view. You will see very busy docks, a cruise terminal, the reconstructed Fort Caroline, the U.S. Naval Station, as well as some beautiful homes. Robert Wilder's quote above is still appropriate today, but "tortuous" could better be replaced by "hectic, fast-paced, frenetic."

Past Trout River, the St. Johns' course turns east. Boaters soon begin to see the massive Dames Point Bridge up ahead. The bridge, also known as the Napoleon Bonaparte Broward Bridge (after a former governor from Duval County) or Dame Point Bridge, is two miles long and rises 175 feet above the main channel of the river. It connects I-95 with Florida Highway 9A. It is the country's longest cable-stayed bridge, carries six lanes of traffic, and is capable of withstanding hurricane-force winds. It opened for highway traffic in 1989, the same year its lighting design won an international competition for beauty.

Just east of Dames Point Bridge is the Yellow Bluff State Historic Site, but because it is more easily visited by land we will discuss that in the second part of this chapter.

On some older maps of the area, you will see that one of the islands under the bridge is Quarantine Island, a name that hearkens back to the times when Jacksonville officials, fearful of the danger of diseases like yellow fever spread by incoming visitors, would quarantine suspected ships until medical personnel could clear the ships. The island has disappeared on modern maps, either because it was joined to the larger Bartram Island or because chamber of commerce officials have euphemized it to Crab or William.

When we reached Blount Island on the north side with its vast number of cars waiting to be sent elsewhere, we went straight ahead on the cutoff rather than on the much longer route to the north around the island. Although our navigation chart showed that the river bends north around Blount Island, low bridges block the passage and force ships and boats to use the "Dames Point Fulton Cutoff Range" to the south of the island. The area north of the island is actually restricted.

Blount Island, which is a major storage area for imported cars, enabled officials to move similar facilities further down the river from their previous location in Talleyrand. The island is better because it is closer to the mouth of the St. Johns. This allows ships to cut down on

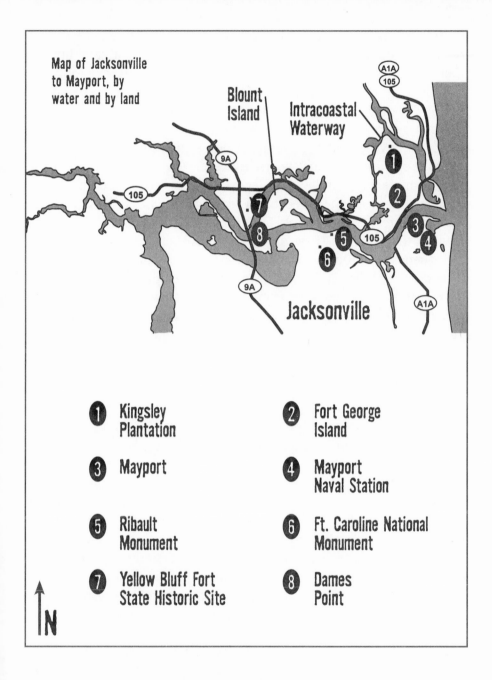

Map of Jacksonville to Mayport, by water and by land

Blount Island

Intracoastal Waterway

Jacksonville

1 Kingsley Plantation

2 Fort George Island

3 Mayport

4 Mayport Naval Station

5 Ribault Monument

6 Ft. Caroline National Monument

7 Yellow Bluff Fort State Historic Site

8 Dames Point

N

the time needed to reach the offloading area. Its location near I-295 and the Dames Point (Broward) Bridge allows shippers to move the cars onto interstate highways without having to contend with urban traffic, and the distance from the industrial area will cut down on the damage done to cars from pollution. Several automobile officials, claiming that industrial pollution from Jacksonville's factories damaged their cars' finishes when the cars were stored closer to the downtown, left the city for Brunswick, Georgia. The new car-storage facility on Blount Island helped make Jacksonville the largest car importer on the east coast.

The large area to the south of the Dames Point Fulton Cutoff Range, Mill Cove, is very shallow, averaging one to two feet in depth, which makes it off limits to most boats. However, the entrance to the Cove between markers 43 and 45 has depths that can accommodate boats.

We soon came upon the reconstructed Fort Caroline on the south bank. The fort's history began on April 30, 1562, when three ships arrived at the mouth of the St. Johns. They carried French soldiers under the command of Huguenot Jean Ribault, who came looking for a place to establish a settlement for other Huguenots, who were seeking religious freedom. The French also needed a site from which to challenge or attack Spanish treasure ships returning to Europe laden with treasure. Upon arrival, the French planted a marker claiming the land for France. They called the river—which earlier Spanish explorers had named *Río de Corrientes* or "River of Currents" because of the water's rapid speed—the River of May (*Rivière de Mai*).

Ribault left temporarily, and in 1564, another French force, led by René de Goulaine de Laudonnière (who had accompanied Ribault on his previous expedition), arrived at the River of May and built a village and the fort on the south bank. They named the village La Caroline and the fort Fort Caroline after French king Charles IX. The fort was triangular in shape and located on the flat land next to the river. The French built it out of timber with a moat on the two sides away from the river. They built a large gate and put on it the arms of France and of their patron, Admiral Coligny. They placed the munitions inside the fort, as well as some houses, but most of their houses were outside the walls.

Unlike Ribault and his crew, who had established good relations with the local Native Americans, the three hundred French in this expedition quarreled with them. Without help or food from the locals, the French soldiers soon were facing starvation for a variety of reasons: they were more interested in looking for gold and silver than in planting crops; they depended on local Native Americans, who could produce enough food for themselves, but not for an extra three hundred mouths; the French were hoping that steady supplies of food would arrive from France, but that did not occur.

Just as they were about to leave for France in August 1565, Ribault arrived with a relief expedition of supplies and six hundred soldiers and settlers, including women and children. Soon afterwards, the French, emboldened with the arrival of Ribault, made plans to oust the Spanish, who had just founded nearby St. Augustine in June 1565 under the leadership of Pedro Menéndez de Avilés. However, while waiting for a high tide off the St. Augustine bar to carry out their operation, the French ships were hit by a sudden storm, driven south, and shipwrecked.

Menéndez used the opportunity to march his men overland to Fort Caroline, which they took by surprise and captured. The Spanish soldiers massacred 140 settlers, sparing about sixty women and children, while about fifty others escaped, including Laudonnière, and sailed back to France. Menéndez then took his men south to Matanzas, where they slaughtered the remnants of the French who had survived the shipwrecks. (*Matanzas* means "slaughter" or "massacre" in Spanish.) The French were thus driven out of Florida, and the Spanish were again in control. In April 1568, the French returned, attacked, and burned the fort that the Spanish had captured from them. The French killed hundreds of Spaniards in the surprise attack and then sailed back to France. Spanish soldiers rebuilt the fort but abandoned it in 1569.

Today, visitors can tour a replica of Fort Caroline. The original fort slid into the St. Johns when erosion along the banks cut into both sides of the river. Archaeologists have not discovered the original site of the fort, partly because the boat traffic on the river precludes extended diving and exploration. Boaters can tie up along the dock and visit the Fort Caroline National Memorial (see details in chapter 10). This is my favorite fort along the river, partly because of its spectacular location overlooking the St. Johns, because of its peaceful setting (there have seldom been more than a few visitors when I have been there), its tasteful visitor center, and the speculation it always evokes. You wonder how different Florida's history would have been if the French had beaten the Spanish here, or if a hurricane had not shipwrecked the French fleet off St. Augustine. Of particular interest inside the visitor center is the original Native American owl totem found at Hontoon Island in 1955 (see chapter three). On either side of the totem are large murals depicting what life may have been like for the Timucuans a thousand years ago.

After we continued east, about two and a half miles past Blount Island, the Intracoastal Waterway comes into the river at an angle from the north and proceeds south at an angle off the river and somewhat east of

Mayport Naval Station can house and repair carriers.

where it came in. You need to pay attention to the signs in the river here since, with so much traffic, boaters can miss the Intracoastal or the continuation of the St. Johns. Even in broad daylight with good charts, we had a difficult time discerning the Intracoastal from the river. In poor visibility, or at night, it must be extremely difficult to make the distinction, especially with ships coming and going. Also look out for the auto ferry that crosses the river on a regular basis, as it cuts directly across the channel throughout the day.

Off on the south bank, we saw a massive aircraft carrier being refurbished in a dry dock that is part of the Mayport Naval Station, which has been in operation since 1942 and whose main facilities are located around the Mayport Basin. If you look carefully to the west of the Naval Station, i.e. to the west of the Naval Station's runways, you can see the St. Johns River Lighthouse. The lighthouse was first authorized by Congress in 1828, just seven years after the Spanish ceded Florida to the United States. Engineers built the tower in 1830 near where the south jetty begins. When erosion weakened it, workers tore it down and built a second one in 1835 about a mile up the river. When officials realized that the 1835 structure was in danger of falling into the river because of erosion around its base, engineers built the present structure still further up the river in 1859. They raised it fifteen feet in 1887 to make it more usable.

The third structure did not succumb to erosion, but was replaced in 1929 by a lightship off Mayport that enabled ships coming into the harbor to be guided more accurately. When the U.S. Navy built Mayport Naval Station in 1941, it suggested that the St. Johns Lighthouse be razed to eliminate what it called a minor hazard to its airplanes, but angry residents successfully prevented that from happening. In 1954, the St. Johns Light Station, a modern beacon light on the eastern edge of the naval station, replaced the lightship. Boaters on the St. Johns cannot see this particular structure because it is much closer to the Atlantic Ocean and southeast of the Naval Station. The Navy made extensive repairs to the old St. Johns Lighthouse and helped place the structure on the National Register of Historic Places in 1982.

The two lighthouses are quite different. The older one, the St. Johns River Lighthouse, which local residents refer to as the Mayport Lighthouse, is a brick conical tower eighty feet tall. The light was turned off in 1929, and the lighthouse was abandoned, but it has remained standing and may become the centerpiece of a museum. The St. Johns Light Station is about a mile away, close to the Atlantic Ocean. The angular, monolithic structure is topped by a small, drum-shaped lantern sixty-four feet above the ground. It still operates, but more for ships in the ocean rather than on the river.

Mayport, on the south shore of the St. Johns and extending from east of the Intracoastal Waterway to the Atlantic, is a busy town with the auto ferry,

A fishing boat on the way home has lots of company.

commercial fishing boats, a gambling cruise ship, seafood restaurants, boat facilities, the Mayport Naval Station, and the headquarters for the pilots who guide the large ships in and out of Jacksonville and its facilities. The name of the town commemorates the "River of May," as the French called the St. Johns in 1562.

According to *Slavery and Plantation Growth in Antebellum Florida, 1821–1860*, laws were passed in the 1850s to try to prevent the escape or theft of slaves. One such regulation in 1854 forced ship captains to anchor at Mayport before putting out to sea. There, officials would board and search the ships. If the officials found any slaves on the ships without written permission from the slave owners or overseers, they would take the slaves and place them in jail in Jacksonville. The captain or owner of the vessel would have to pay the expenses associated with removing the slaves from the vessels and placing them in jail. Captains or owners who did not follow the regulations or interfered with the search parties were subject to fines of $500 to $2,000. The searching officers kept careful records of all ships leaving or arriving in Jacksonville, and received $2.50 for each ship boarded and searched, which the captain or ship owner paid.

Just north of Mayport across the St. Johns is Fort George Island, named after Fort St. George, which Georgia's General James Oglethorpe built in preparation for an eventual assault on St. Augustine in 1740. The fort, which no longer exists, was primarily an earthwork enclosed within a palisade.

Fort George Island was the site of slaveowner Zephaniah Kingsley's main plantation. Kingsley had plantations on the St. Johns River from Drayton Island north (see chapter seven for information on his plantation at Laurel Grove). He operated his Fort George property from 1813 to 1839. His wife, Anna Madgigaine Jai, was a princess from Madagascar whom he purchased as a slave and freed in 1811. She assisted him in the operation of the plantation. Kingsley trained his slaves to be skilled workers, which increased their value and his profits from their sale. Although he did not advocate the abolition of slavery and, in fact, remained a slave-owner until he died, Kingsley allowed his slaves to work at a craft or tend their own gardens once they had completed the required labor for the day. The slaves could usually keep the proceeds from the sale of produce or craft items.

After Florida became part of the United States in 1821, Congress passed laws that discriminated against free blacks and put harsh restrictions on African slaves. That prompted Kingsley to move his family to Haiti, where his and Anna's descendants live today. Kingsley returned to Fort George Island, where he was appointed postmaster and justice of the peace for Duval County. Today, the National Park Service administers the Kingsley Plantation and offers tours of the plantation house, kitchen house, barn, and the ruins of twenty-five slave cabins (see chapter 10 for visiting information).

Continuing east on the St. Johns, we approach the Timucuan Ecological and Historic Preserve. The 46,000-acre preserve encompasses much of the land between the St. Johns and Nassau Rivers. It was established in 1988 to protect one of the last unspoiled coastal wetlands on the Atlantic Coast and to preserve historic and prehistoric sites within the area. Its estuarine ecosystem includes salt marsh, coastal dunes, and hardwood hammocks, all rich in native vegetation and animal life. Among the bird life here one can find bright orange summer tanagers, gulls, brown pelicans, and painted buntings. Other animal life includes marsh rabbits and sea turtles. Archaeological evidence indicates 6,000 years of human habitation in the area. The Timucuan Preserve has within its boundaries federal, state, and city park lands, as well as more than three hundred private landowners.

In 1996, as part of its ongoing land-acquisition program, the Nature Conservancy, in partnership with the city of Jacksonville, the Florida Department of Environmental Protection, the National Park Service, and the St. Johns River Water Management District, bought more than one thousand acres of uplands just north of the St. Johns in the Pumpkin Hill Creek area. The parcels contain scrubby flatwoods and some of the last maritime hammocks close to urban Jacksonville and are part of the Timucuan Preserve.

The Theodore Roosevelt and Cedar Point areas provide the visitor with access to the marine estuarine environment and surrounding coastal forest for hiking, nature observation, birding, and photography. Walking trails provide opportunities for visitors to see an abundance of wildlife. While we saw different kinds of birds, we heard others signaling to each other or just singing away. Visitor signs also told us to be generous with the insect repellant and to watch out for snakes.

Finally, we come near the Mayport Naval Station. In operation since 1942, today the station can handle thirty-four ships and has an eight-thousand-foot-runway on which most airplanes can land. The facility has 3,400 acres and is the third largest naval facility in the continental United

States. Approximately 14,000 active-duty personnel, 45,000 family members and retirees, and 1,400 civilian employees work at or live near the Mayport facility.

This final part of the river is the most harrowing with a mixture of freighters, tugs, Navy vessels, pleasure boats, fishing boats, etc. The jetties stretch out for about a mile on each side of the channel leading to and from the Atlantic, and buoys mark the ship channel for another mile out to sea. Before engineers built the jetties here, nor'easters could play havoc with the channel at the mouth of the river. Those using small or slow boats need to be aware of the strong tidal currents to and from the ocean.

On the south side of the river, just before the jetties, is the wide and deep channel reserved for Navy vessels. The Navy dredged the basin, called Ribault Bay or Mayport Basin, in 1950, built a carrier pier, then built a second carrier pier in 1954. The restricted basin is off-limits to non-Navy boats, although such boats in a dire emergency have been known to use it for a short time. Severely damaged boats in danger of sinking should not use the basin but should instead head for Ward's Bank on the northern shore of the river, where they can beach and perhaps be salvaged. Among the carriers that have docked in Mayport have been USS *Lake Champlain,* USS *Franklin D. Roosevelt,* USS *Shangri La,* USS *Saratoga,* and USS *Forrestal.* During the Cuban Missile Crisis of 1962, Mayport became the advance staging area for the Second Marine

Container ships deliver goods to the docks above Jacksonville.

Division and supported many vessels, including five aircraft carriers. The fact that the Navy built a huge Trident submarine base at Kings Bay, Georgia, to the north of Mayport, not only brought in more military facilities to the area, but generated much ongoing income to North Florida.

Boaters coming into the river at night from the Atlantic and not wishing to go further up toward Jacksonville need to take care when they anchor since large ships using the channel through the night can cause strong wakes that might dislodge anchored boats. Mayport has facilities for docking overnight that include floating docks and concrete pilings.

O n the west and north side of the river. North of the center of Jacksonville, cross Trout River on I-95/SR 9 and then take a right on SR 105 (Heckscher Drive). The Jacksonville Zoological Gardens is off to the right with a wide diversity of animals. The easiest way to get to Heckscher Drive, although it does involve going through the center of the city, is to take highway 17, which goes from Palatka through Jacksonville to North Florida.

by land from Jackson- ville to Mayport

SR 105 (Heckscher Drive) goes along the river across several small bridges around Blount Island, a very busy industrial site. It passes the U.S. Naval Reservation, Broward River, and Dunn Creek. Dames Point Park off Florida 9A at the Heckscher Drive exit is a good place from which to view the Dames Point Bridge. Immediately west of the 9A interchange on Heckscher is the intersection with New Berlin Road. Head south (towards the bridge) on New Berlin Road. Drive less than a mile to the intersection of Dames Point Road. Turn right onto Dames Point Road, then left under the bridge to the end of the road, where the park is next to the river; the park is actually directly under the bridge.

At the intersection of Dames Point Road and New Berlin Road, turn right and go .3 miles to Yellow Bluff State Historic Site on the right before you come to the river. The fort, which is very easy to miss and which has to be the least ostentatious facility of its kind in the area, was part of a series of forts built for the defense of the river during the Civil War. Both Confederate and Union forces occupied the fort at different times. Displayed at the entrance to the earthenworks is a series of documents from official records.

A small moat surrounds the fort.

Heckscher Drive continues to the east around Blount Island over Little Marsh Island, and then Fort George Island, the site of the Kingsley Plantation (see above). Past the place where the toll ferry takes cars across the river is Huguenot Memorial, a relatively new, undeveloped park which commemorates the landing of Jean Ribault and a group of Huguenot refugees from France in the 1560s. You can drive out to the beach and up to the jetty that borders the northern side of the river out into the ocean. The view of passing freighters and small boats, as well as of Mayport across the river, is worth the drive out to the beach. The park is located on Fort George Island and has several miles of beach for walking and swimming. It is the only park in Duval County that allows driving on the beach, except for a no-vehicles zone about five hundred feet long. The park has waterfront campsites, a bird observation area, and excellent views of the river and the ocean. The park also offers swimming, fishing, surfing, a boat launch area, picnic shelters, restrooms, and shower facilities. The Florida Fish and Wildlife Conservation Commission has designated the park a Great Florida Birding Trail site because of the outstanding habitat and the abundance of birds of various kinds, for example bar-tailed godwits, gannets, loons and sea ducks, shorebirds, and terns.

No highway parallels the river through Jacksonville on the eastern shore, but the area has many residential areas. From Mandarin, when I want to avoid eastern Jacksonville, I take 295 to 95 to 115 to 10 and follow signs to Fort Caroline. From Dames Point Bridge, drivers can go east on Fort Caroline Road through Beacon Hills to Fort Caroline National Monument, which is definitely worth a visit, especially if you can combine it with a short drive to the Ribault Monument to the east overlooking the river.

About a mile away to the east of the Fort Caroline National Memorial, and reached more easily by car than by walking, is the Ribault Monument, a replica of the stone column that Jean Ribault placed at the mouth of the River of May on May 2, 1562. By erecting the original monument, Ribault claimed the land for France and vowed to return and settle the land. Before leaving, he inspected a high bluff, now called St. Johns Bluff, as a possible site for the planned French colony.

East of the Ribault Monument and next to the St. Johns is Dredge Spoil Island, which the Jacksonville Port Authority controls. It is technically an island because small streams surround it. We could see vehicles on the island, spreading the sand around and leveling out the island. We remembered how important dredging was to the successful use of the waterway by Mayport since the sand bar there effectively blocked large ships from entering and leaving the river until engineers successfully dredged the river and later built the jetties into the ocean. Midway between the fort and the monument is Spanish Pond, which the Spanish supposedly trekked through on their way to capturing Fort Caroline. A one-mile-long trail leads through the swamp. (Don't forget plenty of drinking water, good shoes, and insect repellant.)

To get to the Atlantic from Fort Caroline, take Mt. Pleasant Road east to McCormick Road to Girvin Road to Atlantic Boulevard east to A1A, then north to Kathryn Abby Hanna Park north of Atlantic Beach. The park honors the author of *Florida, Land of Change* (1941) and co-author of *Lake Okeechobee: Wellspring of the Everglades* (1948) and *Florida's Golden Sands* (1950) who served on the board of Parks and Historical Places. In the 1940s investor/millionaire Winthrop Bancroft donated five acres of beachfront property to the city of Jacksonville as the nucleus of Hanna Park, which today has trails for off-road biking, walking, and hiking; freshwater and saltwater fishing; playgrounds, and clean beaches. It also has

The Ribault Monument marks the place where the French came ashore in 1562.

250 campsites and accommodates both tent campers and recreational vehicles. The park also has climate-controlled cabins.

Further up the road is Mayport Naval Station, which is not open to the general public, but occasionally the public is invited to special events there. The events are announced in the local media and on the base's recording at (904) 270-NAVY.

To get to Mayport, go back to A1A (Mayport Road) and follow it across the Timucuan Ecological and Historic Preserve to the little town of Mayport, where you can take the car ferry (fee) across the St. Johns and continue on A1A on the northern side of the river. Mayport has several restaurants and boat facilities.

Conclusion

When we reached the stone breakwater at Mayport and headed into the Atlantic, the water became appreciably rougher, what with the waves coming into us, the large ships and fishing boats passing us, and the wind picking up. As the waves actually came over the bow of our boat, we turned back, retraced our path to Jacksonville, and spent the night in a hotel. My friends continued on the next day to Mayport and down the Intracoastal Waterway to their home in Indialantic, and I returned to Gainesville.

We had done what we had set out to do: boat the whole St. Johns, go up some of her creeks and lakes, talk to people along the way, quietly observe as much wildlife as possible, and learn as much as we could about the history, ecology, and future of Florida's most important river.

I couldn't help but thinking that, in a way, Florida's beautiful coastline with its sand and white beaches has saved rivers like the St. Johns from even more exploitation than they would have experienced if visitors/settlers had preferred the interior of the state. True, nineteenth-century visitors went by steamboat up the St. Johns to Silver Springs and Blue Spring and Sanford, but, in general, they preferred to settle along the coastline of the state, especially in the southern half of Florida—just as newcomers do today. Such a preference has spared the interior and its rivers from the garish excesses of so many ocean and Gulf communities.

I want to end this travelogue with some personal observations. First, I must note how much of the history of Florida has taken place along the St. Johns. Beginning with the early mastodons, on to the Native Americans, European explorers, settlers, and finally today's tourists, the river has seen thousands of years of history. As we followed the river, how often I thought of the Timucuans living at Mount Royal; of John and William Bartram canoeing the streams; of Zephaniah Kingsley managing his slaves at several plantations; of Harriet Beecher Stowe sitting on her porch at Mandarin waving to the steamboats passing by; of Marjorie Kinnan Rawlings finding herself on her river sojourn.

I also realized just how fragile the river is. I think of how many times people have ignored history and introduced exotics like the water hyacinth into the river's waters, polluted the water by dumping toxic chemicals, and built wherever they wanted regardless of damage to the environment. Thank goodness for the watchdog groups and conservationists who are determined to save this beautiful river for future generations.

Finally, I reflect on how spectacularly beautiful the river is, especially in the offshoots and quiet streams leading off the main channel, or the uninhabited stretches, or in the great abundance of wildlife we saw. If you want to see what Florida must have looked like a thousand years ago, take a trip on the St. Johns.

Appendices

Information for Boaters

Take care when you plan a trip on the St. Johns. From June through September you are liable to experience afternoon showers which can be quite severe. Most of the traffic on the river is in the daytime. Cruising the river at night, especially in the unmarked parts of the southern river, is just too dangerous because of hidden stumps in the river, sharp bends, and even alligators. The river is very busy on weekends.

Use sun block each day since, even in winter, the sun's reflection off the water can cause a nasty burn, and Florida leads the nation in skin cancer. Wearing a hat, especially one that covers the ears, is a good idea (each day on a boat will probably be a "bad hair" day anyway because of the breeze). Drink lots of water, even when you are not thirsty. Insect repellant is a must, especially for those who want to camp out.

Recommended boat equipment, besides the usual safety equipment, is a depth finder because of all the hidden trees and obstacles in the opaque water, as well as a radio that boaters can use in case of trouble, especially on the large lakes during a sudden storm. If you are canoeing or kayaking in remote areas of the river, place a tall, bright warning flag on your boat to be more visible above the high grasses, especially for motorboats and airboats. You might want to avoid paddling in remote areas during alligator mating season in the spring since the reptiles can get overly active at such times. Don't take any small pets in canoes or kayaks since they are a favorite meal of gators.

Among the necessary items for a trip on the river is a set of good maps. I found most useful a set of three maps (maps 314, 331, and 332) available from Kingfisher Maps, Inc., 110 Liberty Drive, Clemson, SC 29631. Phone 800-326-0257. Fax 864-654-2208. www.kingfishermaps.com. The maps are GPS compatible, have marine listings, road markings, and lake structures noted.

If you plan to tent along the way or stay in motels, take all your food off the boat. If not, the ever-present raccoons will get at it. Some of them apparently can read, since they opened only the box labeled "lunch" on our boat.

Note that fishing in freshwater rivers and lakes requires a license for those under the age of 60.

Places to Visit, Stay, and Eat

Below you will find a list of places to visit, stay, and eat along the St. Johns, arranged alphabetically within each chapter. This list is not exhaustive. To find the most up-to-date and accurate information, we recommend that you consult with the chambers of commerce or tourism bureaus for the cities or counties you will visit; their contact information is also provided below.

1. St. Johns Marsh to Lake Monroe

- Camp Holly offers air boat rides, boats, canoes, ramp, bait, tackle, and snacks. A sign ("No shoes, No shirt, No Problem") indicates the informality of the restaurant. On US 192, 3 miles west of I-95 at the bridge over the St. Johns River, west of Melbourne. 321-723-2179.
- Gator Landing Riverside Grille at the Sanford Boat Works and Marina at SR 415 east of Sanford. 407-322-2150.
- Lemon Bluff Campground offers camping and a boat ramp. 949 Lemon Bluff Road, Osteen, FL. 407-322-1279.
- Lone Cabbage Fish Camp sells bait and tackle and has airboat rides. SR 520 at St. Johns River, 4 miles west of I-95, at the Orange and Brevard County lines west of Cocoa. 321-632-4199. www.twisterairboatrides. com
- The Museum of Geneva History, which is on the west bank of Lake Harney, is open on the first Sunday of each month, October to April, 2–4 p.m. and by appointment. 165 First Street, Geneva. 407-349-5495. www.usgennet.org/usa/fl/county/seminole/geneva
- Three Forks Marsh Conservation Area, west of Melbourne, 321-752-3115.

2. Sanford to Hontoon Island

- The Beresford Lady boat has brunch and buffet cruises. Lake Beresford. 888-740-7523. http://www.orlandotouristinformationbureau.com/eco-tours/river_boat.htm
- Best Western Marina Hotel and Conference Center Inn is on the Sanford waterfront. Boaters can tie up along the waterfront. 530 North Palmetto Avenue, Sanford. 407-323-1910.
- Big Tree County Park. 761 General Hutchinson Parkway, Longwood. 407-788-0405. http://www.seminolecountyfl.gov/guide/parks/park1.asp

- Blue Spring State Park has food, lodging, camping, boat rentals, toilets and showers, groceries, ice, snacks, and water. The state park is located at 2100 West French Avenue, Orange City. 386-775-3663. http://www.floridastateparks.org/bluespring/default.asp
- Boat Show Marina can accommodate boats up to 70', has slips, moorings, and electricity; has lift capacity for 35-ton boats; can perform repairs on hulls, motors, and radios; has a boat ramp, pump-out station, food, toilets, showers, and boat storage; and sells ice, snacks, water, hardware, and boat gas. North of Whitehair Bridge, DeBary. 386-736-6601.
- Central Florida Zoo. 3755 N.W. Highway 17-92 at I-4 (Exit 104), Sanford near Lake Monroe. 407-323-4450. http://www.centralfloridazoo.org/home.htm
- DeBary Hall offers guided tours; special group tours can be arranged. Can be used for weddings, festivals, and corporate retreats. 210 Sunrise Boulevard, DeBary. 386-668-3840 or 386-736-5953. www.debaryhall.com
- DeLeon Springs State Recreation Area. At the corner of Ponce de Leon Blvd. and Burt Parks Road in De Leon Springs. 386-985-4212. http://www.abfla.com/parks/DeLeonSprings/deleon.html You can rent boats there and have a meal at the Old Spanish Sugar Mill Grill and Griddle House, 386-985-5644.
- Ed Stone Park has toilets and water. Near Whitehair Bridge, DeBary. 386-734-0581.
- Gemini Springs County Park. 37 Dirksen Drive, DeBary. 386-668-3810. http://volusia.org/parks/gemini.htm
- Greater Sanford Chamber of Commerce has brochures on the area. 400 East First Street, Sanford.
- Highbanks Marina and Camp Resort has 200 RV sites, 2300' river frontage, pontoon boat rentals, a swimming pool, cabins for rent, a 72-slip marina, a pump-out station, toilets, showers, and laundry, boat storage, boat gas, country store, bait and tackle shop, and wildlife boat tours. 488 W. Highbanks Road, DeBary. 407-330-1612 or 386-668-4491. Restaurant: Swamp House Grill. 386-668-8891. www.campresort.com
- Highland Park Fish Camp/Marina can accommodate boats up to 24'; has slips and electricity, boat storage, a boat ramp, boat rentals, lodging and camping, toilets and showers; sells ice, snacks, water, hardware, tackle, and boat gas. Located between Hontoon Island and DeLeon

Springs at 2640 W. Highland Park Road, DeLand. 800-525-3477 or 386-734-2334. www.hpfishcamp.com

- Manatee Seeker Scenic Cruise on the St. Johns is a two-hour, fully narrated tour about the wildlife in the area. The boat leaves from Pier 44 Marina at the SR 44 bridge, DeBary. 1-800-587-7131. www.vis-arts. com/manatee
- Rivership Romance Tours go around Lake Monroe and along the St. Johns River on this double-decked ship. Tours leave from 433 North Palmetto Avenue, Sanford. Luncheon and dinner cruises available. 800-423-7401 or 407-321-5091. ww.rivershipromance.com
- St. Johns River Eco Tours has a two-hour narrated tour of the wildlife. It leaves from Blue Spring State Park at 2100 West French Avenue, Orange City. 407-330-1612 or 386-917-0724. www.sjrivercruises.com
- Safari River Tours, Inc. has tours departing from Highbanks Marina & Camp Resort and from DeLeon Springs Park. 222 Lucerne Drive, Debary. 386-668-4491 or 386-740-0333 or toll free 877-740-0333 [YES]. www.safaririvertours.com
- Sanford Museum along the Sanford waterfront has many displays about the history of the area. 520 East First Street, Sanford. 407-302-1000. http://www.ci.sanford.fl.us/cf03.html
- Thursby House. Contact Blue Spring State Park (see above).
- Tropical Resort and Marina has a convenience store, gift shop, laundry facilities, pool, boat launch, waterfront campsites, fully equipped efficiency suites, slips for boat rentals, pontoon rentals, and fishing boat rentals. 1485 Lakeview Drive, Lake Beresford. 386-734-3080. http://hometown.aol.com/tropmarina

3. Hontoon Island through Astor

- Astor Bridge Marina is a newly restored complex with riverfront cottages, canal front motel rooms, boat dockage, bike storage, ramp use, even call-ahead takeout food. 1575 W. Highway 40 at the Astor Bridge. 386-749-4407 or toll free 866-BDPOTTS. www. astorbridgemarina.com
- Bean's Bar-B-Que, which is next to Front Street Bait & Tackle in Astor (see below) on the west side, has takeout ribs, chicken, pork, and beef. Open only Saturday and Sunday. 352-759-2795.
- Blackwater Inn serves lunch and dinner, and has restaurant docking. Located at SR 40 and the bridge over the river at Astor. 352- 759-2808. http://www.florida-secrets.com/Restaurants/NE/Blackwater.htm

- Blair's Jungle Den about one-half mile north of the Highway 40 bridge in Astor, has gasoline, a boat ramp, campground, sanitary disposal center, restrooms, snack bar, rental cabins, electrical hookups, picnic area, boat rentals, overnight lodging, and bait and tackle. 1820 Jungle Den Road, Astor. 386-749-2264. www.blairsjungleden.com
- Cactus Key Raw Bar n' Grill serves breakfast, lunch, and dinner. 1820 Ormands Jungle Den Road, next to Blair's Jungle Den, Astor. 386-749-9700.
- Front Street Bait & Tackle in Astor, one-quarter mile south of the bridge on the west side of the river, is a full-service bait and tackle store with cold drinks, ice, snacks, beer, oysters, gator meat, and a variety of seafood. Offers boat rentals and cabins with boat slips. 55522 Front Street, Astor. 352-759-2795.
- Holly Bluff Marina can accommodate boats up to 70'; has slips with electricity; monitors VHF channel 12; has a lift with a capacity of 30 tons; has facilities for repairing hulls, motors, and radios; has a boat ramp, boat rentals, a pump-out station, toilets, showers, laundry facilities, boat storage, ice, snacks, water, hardware, and boat gas. Located near Hontoon Island State Park, DeBary. 1-800-237-5105 or 386-822-9992. http://www.hollybluff.com/.
- Hontoon Island State Park has a tent camping area and cabins for rent; reservations are recommended for both. Docks are available for day use; overnight dockage is available. Fishing is available; a Florida fishing license is required for persons 16 years of age or older. Canoes can be rented. The island is accessible by private boat or by a free ferry from across the river. Visitors can park their cars near the ferry landing and walk down to the dock to be seen by the ferryman across the river. For more information contact the state park at 2309 River Ridge Road, Deland. 386- 736-5309. For camping and cabin reservations at this and any Florida state park, call toll-free at 1-800-326-3521 or visit www.reserveamerica.com
- Hontoon Landing Resort & Marina has boat rentals, a motel with a swimming pool, slips with electricity, a boat ramp and pump-out station, boat rentals, boat gas, food, lodging, groceries, ice, snacks, water, hardware, bait, and tackle. Its marina can handle boats up to 60'. 2317 River Ridge Road, DeBary. 386-734-2474 or 1-800-248-2474. http://www.hontoon.com/.
- Lake Woodruff National Wildlife Refuge. 2045 Mud Lake Road, DeLeon Springs. 386-985-4673. http://lakewoodruff.fws.gov/

- Parramore's Fantastic Fish Camp and Family Resort is located at the head of the old river oxbow on Morrison's Bluff at 1675 S. Moon Road, Astor. 1-800-516-2386. www.parramores.com
- Riverview Cottages can be rented daily, weekly, or monthly. 55530 Front Street, Astor. 877-759-2294. http://www.river37.com.
- Riverview North Lodging can be rented daily, weekly, or long-term. Offers boat slips. 25124 Blackwater Lane, Astor. 352-759-3472. http://www.cottages.org/properties/FL-Astor-RiverviewNorth.htm
- South Moon Fish Camp has gasoline, a boat ramp, restrooms, snack bar, a picnic area, boat rentals, overnight lodging, and bait and tackle. Located at 1977 South Moon Road, above Volusia on the east side. 386-749-2383. http://www.stjohnsrivercountry.com/do/fishing/camps/

4. Lake George to Fruitland

- Deadman's Landing, on the eastern shore of Lake George, has a boat ramp. Located at western end of SR 305 west of Seville, Lake George.
- Georgetown Marina and Lodge has gasoline, a boat ramp, campgrounds, restrooms, a snack bar, overnight lodging, boat lift, boat slips, boat dockage, and bait and tackle. 1533 CR 309, Georgetown. 386-467-2002. http://www.flausa.com/interests/moreinfo.php/ZID23=7507/ListingFormat=fish
- Juniper Springs Recreation Area. On SR 40 22 miles east of Silver Springs. 352-625-3147 or 352-625-2808. For information about canoe rentals, call 352-625-2808 or 352-625-2520.
- Pine Island Resort, Campground, and Marina on the eastern shore of Lake George has gasoline, a boat ramp, campground, sanitary disposal station, restrooms, electrical hookups, boat rentals, and bait and tackle. 1600 Lake George Road, Lake George. 386- 749-2818.
- Salt Springs Recreation Area . 14151 SR 19N, Salt Springs. 352-685-2048. http://www.tfn.net/springs/Salt.htm. Visitors can rent boats and get snacks and fishing supplies at Salt Springs Run Marina & Landing, 25711 NE 134th Place, Salt Springs. 352-685-2255.
- Silver Glen Springs Recreation Area 28 miles east of Ocala on SR 40 and to the west of Lake George has a boat ramp, campground, sanitary disposal station, restrooms, and picnic area. 352-685-2799. http://www.dep.state.fl.us/springs/locator/silverglen.htm.

5. Little Lake George to East Palatka

- Bass Haven Lodge has rooms for rent and a restaurant. 1 Mill Street, Welaka (look out for a very small sign on the river; located north of marker 48 and Anderson's Marina). 386-467-8812 or toll-free 1-866-646-1820. www.basshaven.com
- Caravelle Wildlife Management Area on SR 19 south of Palatka. 352-732-1225. http://www.flausa.com/interests/moreinfo.php/ ZID23 = 14985/ListingFormat = biking
- The Floridian Sports Club is an upscale lodging option that offers cottages and a restaurant. Between markers 42 and 43 on the Welaka side. 386-467-2181. www. floridiansportsclub.com
- Georgia Boys Fish Camp on Dunn's Creek has motel rooms, efficiencies, and cottages for rent as well as boat ramp, gas, boat storage, snacks, and drinks. 217 Butler Drive, Satsuma. 386-325-7764. http://www. floridavacations.com/fv/16290.html
- Lake Ocklawaha Visitors Center. 3199 NE Highway 315, Silver Springs. 352 236-0288. http://www.southernregion.fs.fed.us/florida/contact/ index.shtml
- Lake View Motel. 1004 N. Summit Street, Crescent City. 386-698-1090.
- Marjorie Harris Carr Visitors Center, 200 Buckman Lock Road off SR 19 south of Palatka. 386-312-2273. http://www.dep.state.fl.us/gwt/cfg/
- Rodeheaver Boys Ranch/Battle of Horse Landing Reenactments. 380 Boys Ranch Rd., Palatka. 386-328-1281. http://www.rbr.org/
- Putnam County Tourist Development Council and Chamber of Commerce. 386-328-1503. http://putnamcountychamber.org/
- Sunset Landing Resort and Campground has cabins, a restaurant, RV hookups, fuel, live bait, tackle, a launch ramp, and guide service. 110 River Bend Road, Welaka (marker 51 south of Welaka; look for the Union 76 gas sign). 386-467-2166 for lodge; 386-467-8430 for restaurant. www.sunsetlanding.net
- Three Bananas Restaurant 11South Lake Street, Crescent City. 386-698-2861.
- Welaka National Fish Hatchery offers free admission to visitors. -726 CR 309, Welaka. 386-467-2374. http://southeast.fws.gov/welaka/

6. Palatka To Green Cove Springs

- Big River Adventures. For riverboat charters on the St. Johns River. Located next to the Outback Crab Shack at 8155 CR 13 at Six Mile Marina. 904-501-9002.
- Budget Inn. Corner of Hwy. 17 and Mosely, Palatka. 386-328-1533. www.budgetinnofpalatka.com.
- City of Green Cove Springs City Hall. 229 Walnut Street, Green Cove Springs. Visitors can obtain from the city hall, which is very close to the river, "An ArchTrek of Historic Green Cove Springs," a self-guided walking tour.
- Green Cove Springs Marina three miles south of the city on SR 16 has a large boatyard and a place where boaters can work on their own vessels. 904-284–1811.
- The Moorings at Crystal Cove. Motel, restaurant, and marina. 133 Crystal Cove Dr., Palatka. 386-325-1055. http://www.themooringsat-crystalcove.com
- Outback Crab Shack at Six Mile Marina. 8155 CR 13 North. 904-522-0500.
- Pacetti's Marina. Campground and fishing resort on the St. Johns. 6550 SR 13 North near Trout Creek. 904-284-5356. http://www.pacettirv.com/
- Putnam County Tourist Development Council and Chamber of Commerce. 386-328-1503. http://putnamcountychamber.org/
- Red Bay Marina. 4013 Red Cove Rd., Green Cove Springs. 904-284-1155.
- Reynolds Park Yacht Center. 1063 Bulkhead Road, Green Cove Springs. 904-284-4667. http://www.rpyc.info/facilities.html
- River Park Inn Bed & Breakfast Lodging. 103 South Magnolia Avenue, Green Cove Springs. 904-284-2994. www.riverparkinn.com This facility is close to the river.

7. Switzerland To Mandarin

- Clark's Fish Camp. 12903 Hood Landing Road, Mandarin. For lunch and dinner. 904-268-3474. http://www.realpagessites.com/clarksfish-camp/
- Maple Leaf Shipwreck. http://mapleleafshipwreck.com/

8. Jacksonville

We have not put any places to stay or eat because of the hundreds of such facilities.

• Arlington Marina. 5137 Arlington Road, Jacksonville. 904-743-2628.
• Dames Point Park under Dames Point Bridge has parking, picnic area, pavilion, observation pier, fishing pier, and restrooms. Free. Open during daylight hours. Off Florida 9A at the Heckscher Drive exit; go west of the 9A interchange on Heckscher to the intersection with New Berlin Road. Head south (towards the bridge) on New Berlin. Drive less than a mile to the intersection of Dames Point Road. Turn right onto Dames Point Road. At the end of the road is the park. A web site for the bridge and park is at http://www.mikestrong.com/dames/
• Delius Festival. For information about the annual Delius Music Festival: http://users3.ev1.net/~wbthomp/jaxville.html
• Gate River Run. http://www.gate-riverrun.com/
• Jacksonville Historical Center. 100B Wharfside Way. 904-396-6307. Has exhibits about the area history from its first residents, the Timucua Indians, to its development as a major city; located on the South-bank Riverwalk. Free admission; open afternoons daily; closed major holidays. http://www.ohwy.com/fl/j/jackshis.htm
• Jacksonville Landing. Has restaurants and attractions. Located by the St. Johns River. http://www.jacksonvillelanding.com/
• Jacksonville Port Authority. JAXPORT is a full-service international trade seaport in Northeast Florida, supporting more than 45,000 in the Jacksonville, Florida area. For information about the authority, including cruises out of the city, see http://www.jaxport.com/ Jacksonville University. http://www.ju.edu/
• Jacksonville Zoological Gardens, commonly known as Jacksonville Zoo, 8605 Zoo Rd., Jacksonville. 904/757-4462 Open daily 9 a.m-5 p.m. or 6 p.m. on weekends and holidays in the summer. Closed Thanksgiving and Christmas Day. Admission fee. http://www.jaxzoo.org/home.asp
• Museum of Science & History, 1025 Museum Circle. 904-396-6674. Has artifacts about the history and ecology of the St. Johns River and pre-Columbian Indian cultures. Alexander Brest Planetarium has multimedia shows. Open Monday-Friday, 10am-5pm; Saturday, 10am-6pm; Sunday, 1-6pm. Closed New Year's Day, Easter, Thanksgiving and Christmas Day. http://www.themosh.com/

- Riverwalk. This promenade along the St. Johns River in Jacksonville consists of over a mile of scenic views of the river and restaurants, bars, shops, museums, and a marina. 904 632 5578.
- Rudder Club of Jacksonville, Inc., 8533 Malaga Avenue, Orange Park. 904-264-4094. Sponsors the annual Mug Race between Palatka and Jacksonville. http://www.rudderclub.com/
- Yellow Bluff Fort Historic State Park. 12157 Heckscher Dr., Jacksonville. 904-251-2324. Free. http://www.floridastateparks.org/yellowbluff/

9. Mayport

- Fort Caroline National Memorial. 12713 Fort Caroline Rd., Jacksonville. 904-641-7155. Open All Year 9:00 a.m. to 4:45 p.m. http://www.nps.gov/foca/
- Huguenot Memorial Park.10980 Heckscher Drive at Fort George Inlet. Open daily 8 a.m. to sunset. Fee to enter. For camping reservations, call 904 251-3335. http://www.coj.net/Departments/Parks + and + Recreation/Recreation + Activities/Huguenot + Memorial + Park.htm
- Kathryn Abby Hanna Park. 500 Wonderwood Drive, Jacksonville south of St. Johns River; fee to enter and also to camp and stay in the cabins. 904-249-4700. http://www.coj.net/Departments/Parks + and + Recreation/Recreation + Activities/Hanna + Park/default.htm
- Kingsley Plantation. 13165 Mount Pleasant Road, Jacksonville, at the northern tip of Ft. George Island off Florida A1A. Open daily 9:00 a.m.- 5:00 p.m. 904 251-3537. http://www.cr.nps.gov/goldcres/sites/kingsley.htm
- Mayport Marine. 4852 North Ocean Street, Mayport; located next to the ferry station. Has fuel, supplies, and is near a restaurant. 904-246-8929 or 1-888-467-8682. http://www.safemooring.com/Florida_First_Coast126.html
- Naval Station Mayport. For information on tours and facilities call 904-270-5401 http://www.nsmayport.navy.mil/
- Sandollar Restaurant and Marina, 9716 Heckscher Drive, Jacksonville, across from Mayport. 904-251-2449. http://www.sandollarrestaurantandmarina.net/
- Singleton's Seafood Shack. 4728 Ocean Street, Mayport. 904-246-4442. http://www.gbronline.com/juliusm/singletons/menu1.htm
- Timucuan Ecological and Historic Preserve. 12713 Fort Caroline Road, Jacksonville.904 641-7155. http://www.nps.gov/timu/

Further Reading

- Bartram, William. *Travels Through North & South Carolina, Georgia, East & West Florida* (1791); edited by Mark Van Doren as *Travels of William Bartram*. New York: Dover, 1955.
- Bathe, Greville. *The St. Johns Railroad, 1858 to 1895*. St. Augustine: 1958.
- Bearse, Ray and Anthony Read. *Conspirator: The Untold Story of Tyler Kent*. New York: Doubleday, 1991.
- Beecher, Mrs. Henry Ward. *Letters from Florida*. New York: Appleton, 1879 (written by the wife of a famous preacher while she lived at Rollestown).
- Belleville, Bill. *River of Lakes: A Journey on Florida's St. Johns River*. Athens, GA: Univ. of Georgia Press, 2000.
- Bennett, Charles. *Twelve on the River St. Johns*. Jacksonville: University of North Florida Press, 1989 (esp. pp. 73–87 about John McIntosh).
- Bentley, Altermese Smith. *Georgetown, The History of a Black Neighborhood*. Sanford: Bentley, 1989.
- Berkeley, Edmund and Dorothy Smith Berkeley. *The Life and Travels of John Bartram*. Gainesville: University Presses of Florida, 1982.
- Biddle, Margaret Seton Fleming. *Hibernia: The Unreturning Tide*. New York: Vantage Press, 1974 (a history of the Hibernia area).
- Bishop, Katherine. *Sanford Now and Then*. Sanford: Bishop, 1976.
- Blakey, Arch Fredric. *Parade of Memories: A History of Clay County, Florida*. Clay County Bicentennial Steering Committee, 1976.
- Boswell, Charles. *The America: The Story of the World's Most Famous Yacht*. New York: David McKay, 1967.
- Buker, George E. *Jacksonville: Riverport—Seaport*. Columbia: Univ. of South Carolina Press, 1992.
- Cabell, Branch and A.J. Hanna. *The St. Johns: A Parade of Diversities*. New York: Farrar & Rinehart, Inc., 1943.
- Carr, Archie. *A Naturalist in Florida: A Celebration of Eden*.
- Cusick, James G. *The Other War of 1812: The Patriot War and the American Invasion of Spanish East Florida*. Gainesville: Univ. Press of Florida, 2003.
- DeCzege, A. Wass. *The History of Astor on the St. Johns, Astor Park and the Surrounding Areas*. Astor: Astor Kiwanis Club, 1982.
- Francke, Jr., Arthur. *Early Days of Seminole County, Florida*. Sanford: Seminole County Historical Commission, 1984.

- Francke, Jr., Arthur. *Fort Mellon, 1837–1842*. Miami: Banyan, 1977.
- Fry, Joseph A. *Henry S. Sanford*. Reno, NV: University of Nevada Press, 1982.
- Gannon, Michael V. *The Cross in the Sand: The Early Catholic Church in Florida, 1513–1870*. Gainesville: University of Florida Press, 1965.
- Gannon, Michael V. *Florida: A Short History*. Gainesville: University Press of Florida, 1993.
- Gibson, Lillian Dillard. *Annals of Volusia*. Volusia: R. Alex Gibson, 1978.
- Gibson, Lillian Dillard. *Early Days in Volusia*. Volusia: R. Alex Gibson, 1975 (the memoirs of Barney Dillard).
- Gibson, Lillian Dillard. *Florida Yarns*. St. Johns Press, 1985.
- Gibson, Lillian Dillard. *To Hell 'n Blazes* (Volusia: R. Alex Gibson, 1981).
- Kennedy, Wm. T., editor. *History of Lake County, Florida*. Tavares, FL: Lake County Historical Society, 1988.
- Graff, Mary B. *Mandarin on the St. Johns*. Gainesville: University of Florida Press, 1953.
- Hanna, A.J. *Flight Into Oblivion*. Baton Rouge: Louisiana State University Press, 1999; originally published in 1938 (about John Breckinridge's escape through Florida).
- Harper, editor, Francis. *The Travels of William Bartram* (Naturalist's Edition). New Haven: Yale University Press, 1958.
- Herbst, Josephine. *New Green World*. New York: Hastings House, 1954 (about the careers of John and William Bartram).
- Holland, Keith V., Lee B. Manley, James W. Towart, editors. *The Maple Leaf: an Extraordinary American Civil War Shipwreck*. Jacksonville: St. Johns Archaeological Expeditions, Inc., 1993.
- Howe, ed., M.A. DeWolfe. *Home Letters of General Sherman*. New York: Scribners, 1909.
- Huff, Sandy. *Paddler's Guide to the Sunshine State*. Gainesville: University Press of Florida, 2001.
- Jahoda, Gloria. *The Road to Samarkand: Frederick Delius and His Music*. New York: Scribner's, 1969.
- Johnson, Katherine Burger. *Juniper, That's Me! The History of the Juniper Club: 1909–1993*. No place: No publisher, 1993?
- Kennedy, Stetson. *After Appomattox: How the South Won the War*. Gainesville: University Press of Florida, 1995.
- Kennedy, Stetson. *Jim Crow Guide: The Way It Was*. Gainesville: University Presses of Florida, 1990.

- Kennedy, Stetson. *The Klan Unmasked.* Gainesville: University Presses of Florida, 1990.
- Kennedy, Stetson. *Palmetto Country.* New York: Duell, Sloan & Pearce, 1942.
- Kennedy, Stetson. *Southern Exposure.* Garden City, N.Y., Doubleday & Co., Inc., 1946.
- Lanier, Sidney. *Florida: Its Scenery, Climate, and History. 1875.* Gainesville: University of Florida Press, 1973.
- "Letters of William Cullen Bryant from Florida," *Florida Historical Quarterly,* 14 (April 1936), pp. 255–274.
- McCarthy, Kevin M., editor. *The Book Lover's Guide to Florida.* Sarasota: Pineapple Press, Inc., 1992 (for a description of the books written about and in the different places along the river).
- McCarthy, Kevin M. *Thirty Florida Shipwrecks,* Sarasota: Pineapple Press, Inc., 1992, (pp. 65-67 about the Maple Leaf, pp. 60-63 about the America, pp. 68-71 about the Columbine, 76–79 about the Commodore).
- Medary, Marjory P. *Orange Winter: A Story of Florida in 1880.* New York: Longmans, Green, 1931 (novel about pioneers traveling up the St. Johns to Sanford).
- Michaels, Brian E. *The River Flows North: A History of Putnam County.* Palatka: The Putnam County Archives and History Commission, 1976.
- Milanich, Jerald T. *Famous Florida Sites: Crystal River and Mount Royal.* Gainesville: University Press of Florida, 1999.
- Milanich, Jerald T. *Florida Indians and the Invasion from Europe.* Gainesville: University Press of Florida, 1995.
- Milanich, Jerald T. *Florida's Indians from Ancient Times to the Present.* Gainesville: University Press of Florida, 1998.
- Mueller, Edward A. *Along the St. Johns and Ocklawaha Rivers.* Charleston, SC: Arcadia, 1999.
- Mueller, Edward A. *Ocklawaha River Steamboats.* Jacksonville: E.A. Mueller, c1983.
- Mueller, Edward A. *St. Johns River Steamboats.* Jacksonville: E.A. Mueller, 1986.
- Mueller, Edward A. *Steamboating on the St. Johns: Some Travel Accounts and Various Steamboat Materials.* Melbourne, Fl: Kellersberger Fund of the South Brevard Historical Society, 1980.

- Myers, Ronald L. and John J. Ewel, editors. *Ecosystems of Florida*. Orlando: University of Central Florida Press, 1990.
- Olschki, Leonardo. "Ponce de León's Fountain of Youth: History of a Geographical Myth," *The Hispanic American Historical Review,* vol. 21, no. 3 (August 1941), pp. 361–385.
- Patterson, Gordon. "Ditches and Dreams: Nelson Fell and the Rise of Fellsmere," *Florida Historical Quarterly,* vol. 76, no. 1 (summer 1997), pp. 1–19.
- Poole, Leslie Kemp and Heather McPherson. "Return to the River," *Florida Magazine, The Orlando Sentinel,* July 16, 1995, pp. 8–19 (about the trip of two women to retrace the river trip that Marjorie Kinnan Rawlings took).
- Price, Eugenia. *Margaret's Story.* New York: Lippincott & Crowell, 1980 (a novel about Margaret Seton Fleming and her family in Hibernia from the 1830s to the 1880s).
- Proby, Kathryn Hall. *Audubon in Florida.* Coral Gables, FL: University of Miami Press, 1974.
- Purdy, Barbara. *The Art and Archaeology of Florida's Wetlands.* Boca Raton, FL: CRC Press, 1991, esp. pp. 228–231 about Tick Island.
- Rawlings, Marjorie Kinnan. *Cross Creek.* New York: Scribner, 1942, esp. chapter 22: "Hyacinth Drift."
- Reeder, Mati Belle. *History of Welaka, 1853–1935.* Welaka: s.n., 1976.
- Robison, Jim and Mark Andrews. *Flashbacks: The Story of Central Florida's Past.* Orlando: The Orange County Historical Society and The Orlando Sentinel, 1995.
- Sanders, Brad. *Guide to William Bartram's Travels, Following the Trail of America's First Great Naturalist.* Athens, GA: Fevertree Press, 2002.
- Sanger, Marjory Bartlett. *Billy Bartram and His Green World.* New York: Farrar, Straus & Giroux, 1972.
- Sastre, Cécile-Marie. "Picolata on the St. Johns: A Preliminary Study." *El Escribano: The St. Augustine Journal of History.* Vol. 32 (1995), pp. 25–64.
- Schaal, Peter. *Sanford As I Knew It, 1912–1935.* Sanford: Schaal, 1970.
- Schafer, Daniel L. *Anna Madgigine, Jai Kingsley: African princess, Florida slave, plantation slaveowner.* Gainesville: University Press of Florida, 2003
- Schafer, Daniel L. "'the forlorn state of poor Billy Bartram': Locating the St. Johns River Plantation of William Bartram," *El Escribano: The St. Augustine Journal of History.* Vol. 32 (1995), pp. 1–11.

• Smith, Julia Floyd. *Slavery and Plantation Growth in Antebellum Florida, 1821–1860.* Gainesville: University of Florida Press, 1973.
• Smith, Ryan. "Carpenter Gothic: The Voices of Episcopal Churches on the St. Johns River," *El Escribano: The St. Augustine Journal of History.* Vol. 32 (1995), pp.65–90.
• Spornick, Charles D., Alan R. Cattier, Robert J. Greene. *An Outdoor Guide to Bartram's Travels.* Athens: University of Georgia Press, 2003.
• Stamm, Doug. *The Springs of Florida.* Sarasota: Pineapple Press, Inc., 1994.
• Stowe, Harriet Beecher. *Palmetto Leaves.* 1873; republished by the University of Florida Press, 1968.
• Taylor, Thomas W., editor. *The Florida Lighthouse Trail.* Sarasota: Pineapple Press, 2001.
• Waitley, Douglas. *Best Backroads of Florida. Vol. 1: The Heartland.* Sarasota: Pineapple Press, 2000.
• Wass, Albert. *Deadly Fog at Deadman's Landing.* Astor: Danubian Press, 1979 (a mystery set in the area and written by a local author).
• Wass, Albert. *The History of Astor on the St. Johns, Astor Park and the Surrounding Area.* Astor: Danubian Press, 1982.
• Wattendorf, Bob. "How Fish Osmoregulate to Adapt to Their Environment," *Florida Wildlife,* vol. 45, no. 4 (July–August 1991), p. 24.
• Wermescher, John W. *The Mystery of Turtle Island.* Bloomington, IN: AuthorHouse, 2002 (a children's book about the area near Welaka).
• Wilder, Robert. *God Has a Long Face.* New York: Bantam, 1952.
• Williamson, Ronald. "Little ditch spawned big hopes, vision," *Daytona Beach News–Journal,* July 8, 2000, p. 1C (about the proposed St. Johns–Indian River Barge Canal).
• Wyman, Jeffries. *Dear Jeffie,* edited by George E. Gifford, Jr. Cambridge, MA: Peabody Museum Press, 1978 (a description of the Hibernia area from 1867 to 1874).

Index